fun baby learning games

Activities to Support Development in Infants, Toddlers, and Two-Year-Olds

Sally Goldberg, PhD

Gryphon House
www.gryphonhouse.com

Copyright
©2018 Sally Goldberg

Published by Gryphon House, Inc.
P. O. Box 10, Lewisville, NC 27023
800.638.0928; 877.638.7576 (fax)
www.gryphonhouse.com

Cover photograph courtesy of Shutterstock.com.

Library of Congress Cataloging-in-Publication Data

The cataloging-in-publication data is registered with the Library of Congress for ISBN 978-0-87659-748-4.

Bulk Purchase

Gryphon House books are available for special premiums and sales promotions as well as for fund-raising use. Special editions or book excerpts also can be created to specifications. For details, call 800.638.0928.

Disclaimer

Gryphon House, Inc., cannot be held responsible for damage, mishap, or injury incurred during the use of or because of activities in this book. Appropriate and reasonable caution and adult supervision of children involved in activities and corresponding to the age and capability of each child involved are recommended at all times. Do not leave children unattended at any time. Observe safety and caution at all times.

Dedication

To my friend, Sue Augir:

Thank you so much for steering me in the right direction. It was your special touch of friendship and professionalism that helped me get this book back on track and ready for its final "meant-to-be" destination.

To my husband, Bob Elam:

Thank you for overseeing the "track." It was your generosity and love that supported me in this part of my early childhood work, which is such a meaningful and important part of my life.

Acknowledgments

This book puts early play into a sequenced context. Whatever age or stage your little one is at, you will be able to learn about and then guide your child through it with precision. Guesswork is out, and confidence is in.

This handy resource is here today because of the many helpful people who chipped in with their time, energy, and resources. Marnie Cochran, who was in on the ground level when the book was conceived and begun, played a big role in the formative stage. Thank you, Marnie. Then years later, along came Stephanie Roselli, executive editor at Gryphon House, and she gets the biggest thank-you of all. First, she gave it her scientific touch and then followed that with her genuine stamp of approval.

Thanks also go to the many mothers who tried out the activities, gave me needed feedback, and even posed with their babies for photos. Thank you very much, Corin Wiser and your daughter Hannah, Amber Bloom and your son Tyler, Rayna Spector and your daughter Peri, Guadalupe Griffin and your son Gabriel, Christine Randhawa and your son Liam, Traci Krystyniak and your daughter Rileigh, and Patty Majerus and your son Tommy. Your practical advice, insight, and patient children all helped me a lot!

A finished product looks simple, but there are many dedicated professionals who work behind the scenes to improve quality in every way. Much appreciation goes to Melissa Henninger, content editor, who helped me raise the bar for excellence. Then along came Karen Sommerfeld, copy editor, who took the whole project to the next level with her good eye. Melissa and Karen, thank you both.

Table of Contents

Foreword

I was an absolute sponge for parenting knowledge as I anticipated the birth of my first child. As the publisher of a parenting magazine, the resources available to me were bountiful. I read everything I could get my hands on! It was during this time that I was fortunate enough to meet Dr. Sally Goldberg.

Dr. Goldberg and I had an instant common bond—the aspiration to educate parents on the importance of early childhood education and nurturing. However, I immediately was intrigued by her refreshing perspective on parenting and the true essence of childhood. Her energy and commonsense approach are welcome alternatives to the numerous modish techniques and gadgets that bombard today's parents.

I implemented Dr. Goldberg's creative ideas with my firstborn. My son and I would spend time coordinating household items of the same color, creating musical instruments from plastic spoons and containers, and making our own flash cards. It was a wonderful moment when his prekindergarten teacher credited his advanced skills to the extra time I had spent with him! Now, my youngest son is also exhibiting an advanced skill level in school. Thank you, Dr. Goldberg!

Parents will revel in the fresh approaches offered in this unique "play-and-learn" system. Dr. Goldberg's suggestions are a blessing for both the stay-at-home and working parent. When there no longer seems to be enough time in the day, her activities allow a parent to make the most of the precious moments of child-parent bonding. Dr. Goldberg shows us that we can allow our children to take the initiative in learn-and-play activities. It is a golden opportunity for creative play when the child is more intrigued by the box the toy came in rather than the toy itself. After reading this book, parents and caregivers will discover that their recycling bin is actually a treasure chest of toys waiting to happen. Parents and caregivers alike can teach invaluable skills while investing nothing more than some creativity and time.

Dr. Sally Goldberg is an inspiration to me both as a professional and a parent. To this day, I simply need to take a moment to refer to her writings and once again feel grounded in this whirlwind of new-millennium parenting. Thank you, Dr. Sally, for reminding us what a special gift parenting actually can be!

Victoria L. Grimes
Publisher
Today's Family Magazine

Preface

This book is a theory- and research-based guide to playing with little ones. All activities foster development in one or more of five areas—cognitive, motor, social-emotional, language, and self-esteem; and each one includes information about the activity, how to do it, and why.

Each of the suggested activities has been carefully selected or specially crafted as a stellar way to encourage a particular skill or emerging milestone. Some you may recognize, as they are based on play interactions that have been passed down through the generations. A few are specifically designed for you to create your own unique add-ons. All are there for you to experience in your own way.

Throughout the book you will see that you are the key player. There is no machine that can take your place. You are vitally needed day in and day out to handle properly the wants and needs of the little ones in your care. When even the most challenging situations arise—problems that an outsider would never know how to fix—poof, you solve them. How? Easy. You are the parent, and you know how. Find out more about this concept in the epilogue, "The Power of the Parent."

Many conveniences have come our way in the digital age. However, none has made the process of guiding children through all their years of growth and development any quicker, easier, or less complex. As a matter of fact, the human touch, both male and female, is still exactly as important to children as it ever was.

Introduction

The first three years of life are more important than most people think. They lay the foundation for all of life to come. Surprising as this may sound, research tells us that if a child has high verbal skills by the age of three, she will likely be successful in school by age six. I pass on to you these well-researched and highly valued concepts that appear often in the literature. First is that an enriched early learning environment in the first three to five years sets the stage for later success in school, and second is that the *R*, *S*, and *T* of parenting—reading, singing, and talking to young children—are key. Moreover, of all the input young children receive in the early years, it is high-quality and high-quantity language that seems to play the biggest role.

In the Far East, people plant Chinese bamboo. During the first four years, they water and fertilize the plant with seemingly little or no results. Then in the fifth year, they again apply water and fertilizer, and in five weeks' time the tree grows 90 feet in height. Many people in Asia know this story and see it as a metaphor for personal growth and resilience. It also helps them to understand how important it is to provide an enriched early educational environment for their children in the first five years. While each book you read to your child, each song you sing, or each individual conversation that you have does not in itself make a major impact, taken altogether they have great value and make a world of difference. Your child knows, and now you know too, that enriching her environment on a daily basis is exactly what is needed to give her the best start possible. Taking this important information into account, you have here in sequenced form well-researched and highly recommended activities that are geared specifically for infants, toddlers, and two-year-olds all the way up to age three.

There are five areas of development that emerge both independently and interactively throughout our lifetime—cognitive, motor, social-emotional, language, and self-esteem. Each one is briefly described below. Just as we all need to eat food from each of the five food groups, so it is necessary for a child to participate in activities from each of the five areas of development. While technology can enhance learning in all of these areas, hands-on interactive play is most important. Each activity has been designed to focus on one particular area, but they all affect each other at the same time.

- **Cognitive: learning about the world**
  Through experiencing the environment in different ways, learning occurs. All of it takes place through the five senses—sight, sound, taste, touch, and smell.

- **Motor: using large (gross) and small (fine) muscle movement in a purposeful manner**

  Through gross motor movement, full-body development takes place. Through fine motor muscle movement, finger and hand dexterity emerge. Gross-motor and fine-motor milestones are reached as large-muscle and small-muscle movements become self-initiated.

- **Social-Emotional: having appropriate interpersonal relationships and a growing sense of self**

  Through a series of specific expanding relationships, almost like the concentric circles that form when a pebble hits a pond, a young person's self-concept keeps emerging. First and foremost is the parent-child relationship; that starts the whole ball rolling. What parents do in an ongoing fashion as they react with excitement over each little miracle of their child's unfolding development builds acceptance. In time, sibling relationships form and create strong allegiances followed by the grandparent, aunt, uncle, and cousin connections that instill loyalty. Last but not least are the associations that emerge with close friends of the family and teachers, babysitters, and various caregivers. Those relationships model commitment.

  The major factor related to all of these relationships is that they provide a safe teaching environment. These people, who differ in personality, style, age, and interests, all love the child. Together they form a group that mirrors to her in a safe and protected way the variety of characteristics of people in the outside world.

- **Language: understanding in a receptive way from listening and reading, and expressing actively by speaking and writing**

  Through activities in the cognitive, motor, social-emotional, and self-esteem areas, language expertise emerges. It also arises out of specific reading, singing, and talking activities. The richer the content of language parents and others use with their little ones, and the higher the quality of language they maintain with each other in front of the children, the better a child's language expertise will be.

- **Self-Esteem: starting with self-awareness, it develops into self-worth**

  Similar to language development, self-esteem develops from specific adult input. Here is the key—do whatever you can to make a child feel valued, needed, and important. "Please help me with . . ." and "Thank you for . . ." are perfect examples. The first sentence includes the magic word *please* that shows respect, and the second example has the two magic words *thank you* that convey appreciation. Combine *please* and *thank you* with a valued, needed, and important task, and you have a formula for creating inner strength.

  An extension of this concept is unconditional love. Parents should keep this coming no matter what happens. Back to one of those child-development mantras: "What you think of your child is what she will think of herself."

A Word about the Activities

This book is designed to be a full program of activities for your child. Unlike most other early play-and-learn books, this is a prescriptive program that includes background information about each activity, how to play it, and why it is important. In addition, after each explanation, there is a short reference to research that is related to the described interactions.

The whole book can be used from the point of view of age, stage, or interest, making it ideal for use in fostering typical development, providing early intervention, and adding enrichment. In addition, while maintaining the fun and excitement that go with all general play, each activity is also designed to be individualized. With this book's primary purpose being guidance, each chapter starts with developmental information related to that particular age and stage. All guidelines are based on averages and explained according to commonly accepted descriptions from current educational theory and research.

Although technology is likely to play a role in your child's life, it is by no means necessary at this early level. On the contrary, hands-on, interactive experiences are necessary. These are not only more meaningful to your little one than reacting to a screen, but they are also just as much fun, if not more. In addition, they are an absolute must for well-rounded, normal development. This whole play-and-learn program has been carefully designed around basic cognitive, motor, social-emotional, language, and self-esteem learning opportunities that are missing from most of the high-tech play that is so prevalent and available for young children today. While some experiences with technology are valuable, many are at the same time limiting when it comes to thinking deeply, using fingers and hands, socializing appropriately, listening and speaking, and simply feeling good about yourself from the inside out.

The activities are organized into sections by age range. Within each age range, the activities are ordered by stage of development. To select an activity, first start with the child's age. If your child seems to be developing typically, go directly to the age-appropriate chapter. Find an activity that you think would be fun and beneficial to your child and play it together.

The milestones listed in the age ranges are the ones that are generally accepted by educators to be associated with those ages, but are not restricted to them. Therefore, it is perfectly acceptable to work on milestones from different age groups with your child. If you think your child is functioning either above or below her age range, use the index to find activities that support the appropriate milestones. Because every child is different and because each child develops at a different rate in different areas, you are likely to find some activities in one age group and other activities in a different age group.

Choosing activities by milestones is also excellent for children with special needs. Often they have functioning levels in one or more areas below their age range. If that is the case, you will be able to find appropriate activities easily, without being restricted to the recommended age. In addition, if you are working on a specific milestone and go directly to it in the index, you can be sure that all activities suggested will be beneficial for enhancing that particular milestone.

Even though the activities are presented by age range, most are not limited to that period. Many can be used over and over in the same or different ways as your baby grows. Reading books, singing songs, and playing simple games are all examples of appropriate activities for children all through the early childhood years. What will grow over time is the extent to which your child will be able to participate in the particular activities.

If you are looking to enrich or just enjoy one of the five areas of development—cognitive, social-emotional, motor, language, or self-esteem—start looking for activities in one age range. Then, if the level seems too high or too low for your child, go to that same area of development in another age range until you find a group of activities that you think will be both helpful and fun for your child.

The major purposes of each activity are both playing and learning. Because these two processes go hand in hand, this guided-play program makes it easy for you to find appropriate play activities that will spur your child on toward positive development. Once you start using the activities and establish an enjoyable play routine, you are likely to experience increased parent-child bonding and a growing positive relationship with your child. These early experiences will have a lasting effect on you, your child, and on your whole parent-child relationship.

PART I

Birth to One Year

Before you embark on this wonderful world of guided play, here are four principles of parenting that I think you will especially like. Enjoy them like a little gift, and allow them to enrich your daily parenting during your baby's first year. If you start with them now, parenting in general will become a more effective experience for years to come.

- Play—Have fun!

- Act natural—Be yourself.

- Respond—Pay attention.

- Touch—Hug and hold.

Your pediatrician will get to know your child. So will your child's babysitters, teachers, and other caregivers. However, no one will know your little one better than you. You began developing your expertise from your baby's first day and even before. Probably you know each and every cry and what it means. They are all different: for hunger, thirst, dirty diapers, getting hurt, and needing attention. You certainly know his personality as it has been developing. Your baby is new and different from any other baby ever born, and you have the privilege to watch his uniqueness and individuality unfold each day. Others will have important input and advice for you, but always remember that you are the one who knows the best!

1 Birth to Three Months

The newest member of your family has just arrived. During this exciting time of introduction, keep your parent-child interactions focused on welcoming your baby. In addition, as you play, talk, and create, notice that you are setting up patterns of interaction that will last a lifetime. The task at hand is to give your baby love, attention, respect, and firm but positive guidance right from the start, and you are the exactly right person to do that. Use the whole play-and-learn system to keep finding activity after activity for joyful play, much movement, and a high level of learning. Every aspect of this book has been well-researched, and this first chapter is specifically designed to guide your baby's early development.

As you notice evidence of growth each day, be sure to express your happiness to your baby. Stay with him as much as you can so as not to miss even one little spurt of development. Keep enjoying anything and everything new. However you nurture, love, guide, support, protect, and teach your baby during these first months is exactly what your baby will love.

Build Skills with Play-and-Learn Fun

Start your play in any way that suits you. Go through activities by age range, chapter by chapter, or find an area that you like in one or more chapters and stick with that. You can also look over the following milestones of development and choose activities that go with ones you deem particularly appropriate for your baby for one reason or another. The index lists suggested activities for each milestone.

Milestones of Development

- Responds to sound and touch
- Looks at faces, patterns, and objects
- Follows a moving object with eyes
- Explores surroundings
- Keeps arms and legs bent and fists clenched
- Lifts head and chest while lying on stomach
- Holds head steady while upright
- Cuddles when held
- Responds to voices

- Smiles socially
- Responds to pleasure with vocalizations
- Responds to sounds with vocalizations
- Responds to pleasure with giggles
- Produces random vowel-like sounds
- Responds to loud sounds with vocalizations
- Responds to voices with vocalizations

Time to begin!

Introduce Cognitive Skills through the Five Senses

Rock-a-Bye Baby

Newborn babies love to look at faces, and yours is the most interesting of all. As you cradle your baby, you will note that his eyes are in the exact right position to see your face as clearly as possible.

Behind the Scenes

Sight is the major sense through which learning takes place, and eye contact is the part of this activity that creates your connection. This particular song has its own special way of connecting parents with their newborns. While most parents attribute this connection to the cradled position, now you know that what your baby sees—you—plays the biggest part.

Research Roundup!

According to researchers Teresa Farroni and colleagues, solid eye contact traditionally takes place around one-and-a-half to two months of age. However, interestingly enough, according to their 2002 study published in the *Proceedings of the National Academy of Sciences*, eye contact can start as early as two days after birth.

How to Do It

1. Hold your baby in a cradled position and make eye contact.

2. Get ready to rock him to the following words. As you sing each line and rock, move your baby with the motions as marked.

   Rock-a-bye baby in the tree-top. (Rock your baby)
   When the wind blows, the cradle will rock. (Rock your baby)
   When the bough breaks, the cradle will fall. (Lower your baby)
   And down will come baby, cradle and all. (Lower your baby and bring him back up)

A Rattle

One of the first play sounds most newborns hear is the sound of a rattle. Many rattles used to be made with opaque plastic, but now some are clear so that the baby can see what makes the sound. A soft bell and the clink of keys are also popular.

Materials
Rattle, a soft bell, or keys

Behind the Scenes
Sound is another powerful avenue for learning. Throughout the ages, parents have made whatever simple, soft, and appealing sounds might be available to attract their babies' attention. They often combined items such as shells and beads to clank, jiggle, or make some kind of pleasing sound. Today's rattles come in many different colors, sizes, and shapes and are made from a variety of materials.

Research Roundup!
According to Penelope Leach, a leading child-development expert, in her book *Your Baby & Child: From Birth to Age Five,* each of your baby's senses is in some kind of working order before birth, and they are all ready to go when your baby is born. There may not be much smelling or tasting in the womb, and there is probably too little friction for much sense of touch, but babies can start hearing quite well beginning at about eighteen weeks in utero, according to the Mayo Clinic.

How to Do It

1. Take turns with the rattle, bell, or keys. First shake one and let your baby respond.

2. Encourage your baby to shake it for you to respond.

3. Switch back and forth, playing and creating interesting sounds.

Nursing or the Bottle

Feeding a newborn, whether by nursing or the bottle, is nature's way of helping you bond with your baby. The natural nursing position brings your baby's eyes just the right distance from your face for your baby to see you as clearly as possible. While nursing was the original form for this process and still is often a preference, the bottle is an excellent substitute. It can be used for one or more feedings a day or for all of them.

It is important to hold your baby in the traditional nursing position and to avoid bottle propping whenever possible.

Materials
If bottle feeding, clean bottle and nipple
Breast milk or formula

How to Do It

1. In a cradled position, feed your baby. Enjoy the cuddling and use as much eye contact as possible.

2. Feeding times come often during these early months, and it is this frequency that creates such powerful bonding. It is also the prime opportunity for the parent to learn about the baby.

Behind the Scenes

Breast milk is produced from a mixture of all foods eaten by the mother and, therefore, does not predispose the child to preference for any specific one. As such, it lays the groundwork for openness to future taste development. Very clever on nature's part!

Research Roundup!

According to the American Academy of Pediatrics, human milk is the best possible food for any infant. Its major ingredients are sugar (lactose), easily digestible proteins, and fat—all properly balanced to suit your baby. In addition, breast milk has a perfect amount of enzymes, antibodies, and other valuable ingredients that foster baby health and protect against conditions such as ear infections, allergies, and many childhood diseases. Formulas approximate this amazing combination of nutrients as best as is possible in these three categories: cow's milk, soy, and specialized combinations for infants with identified needs. Much more information about nursing and formulas can be found in the highly respected book *Caring for Your Baby and Young Child: Birth to Age 5*.

Cotton

Because soft is a great texture for newborns, cotton is a natural. You probably already have cotton balls as one of your baby supplies, and the large size is best for this activity.

Materials

Large cotton balls

Behind the Scenes

Remember this old saying? People remember 10 percent of what they hear, 50 percent of what they see, and 90 percent of what they experience. Touching is a huge learning mechanism. Texture books and activities are great for your baby, beginning at this time.

How to Do It

1. Slowly and gently open up your baby's fist.

2. Put a cotton ball inside.

3. Observe your baby's reaction. Your baby is likely to show pleasure from exposure to the soft texture.

Research Roundup!

According to Tiffany Field and colleagues, touch from the caregiver-to-baby point of view improves health and contributes to the treatment of disease. The researchers developed massage therapy as a way to promote healthy weight gain for babies born prematurely.

Flower Scents

Newborns have a well-developed sense of smell. Stimulating that sense is not only appropriate but is also often overlooked. Use fresh flowers if they are available, but you can also substitute dried or silk flowers sprayed with nontoxic scents.

Materials
Fresh or dried flowers with a scent you enjoy
Silk flowers (optional)
Nontoxic scent, such as lemon or lime juice, spices such as
   cinnamon, nutmeg, or garlic (optional)

Behind the Scenes
All learning takes place through the five senses. The more senses are activated, the more powerful the learning experience. Certain smells that a person associates with a particular event can bring back specific related memories.

Research Roundup!
According to smell research as reported by Penelope Leach in her book *Your Baby & Child: From Birth to Age Five*, babies can distinguish between smells and even have a stronger ability to do so than adults. She explains it this way: "If a breast pad worn by his mother is put to one side of a baby's head and a breast pad used by another mother is placed on the other side, the baby will choose the mother smell, turning his head to that side in 75 percent of the trials."

How to Do It

1. Put your baby in a position in which he can comfortably see the flowers.

2. Together, smell them. **Don't hold flowers close to your baby's nose, particularly if they've been sprayed with a scent.** Simply waft them in front of you both so you can smell them from a safe distance.

3. Observe the baby to note his reaction. If he doesn't seem to enjoy the experience, try again another day.

Practice Motor Skills with Small- and Large-Muscle Exercises

Relax-a-Baby

This activity is a well-accepted way to help your newborn open up out of the fetal position. Many people think about only the legs when it comes to unfolding, but all parts of your baby's body need relaxation and stretching to help him adapt to his new and freer environment.

Materials
None

Behind the Scenes
While unfolding and straightening out your baby's limbs is the motor goal for this activity, the secondary bonus is relaxation. To this end, you can rub your baby's feet and hands, add soft music, do gentle massage, and use sweet and loving language.

How to Do It

1. Place your baby facing you on a bed or other soft surface.

2. Pat your baby's arms, legs, and tummy slowly, regularly, and softly. Gradually you will feel your baby's body relax.

3. Slowly open and close your baby's arms crosswise across his chest.

4. Gently push your baby's legs up and down in a pedaling motion, alternating them by holding them under your baby's knees.

5. Try a lengthening motion by moving your baby's arms up and down, first with both arms at the same time and then by alternating them.

6. Go through all of these movements over and over for as long as you both continue to enjoy them.

Research Roundup!

Mildred Carter, an expert in the field of reflexology, says that touch motions on babies' feet and hands provide excellent relaxation input. Carter and coauthor Tammy Weber explain in their book *Body Reflexology: Healing at Your Fingertips* that rubbing a baby on the foot is an effective way to get a crying or colicky baby to go to sleep. The book also reports that a very soft and scratchy movement on the back of the hands with the fingernails is very soothing and usually quiets a restless child.

Open Up

Because a newborn has a reflex grasp, it is helpful to loosen it up. Any convenient, safe item the size of a child's small block can be used for this play. Make sure the object is clean, has more substance to it than cotton, and is too big to be swallowed.

Materials
Small block

Behind the Scenes
From one generation to the next, parents continue to find appealing objects to use for this purpose. No matter the item, the goal of opening up baby's reflexive grasp has stayed the same.

How to Do It

1. Help your baby grasp the item.

2. Gently take it out of your baby's hand.

3. Give the item back to your baby.

4. Take as many turns as you and your baby would like.

Research Roundup!

Research from the University of Maryland Medical Center states that all babies are born with a grasp reflex. "This movement occurs if you place a finger on the infant's open palm; the hand will close around the finger. Trying to remove the finger causes the grip to tighten. Newborn infants have strong grasps and can almost be lifted up if both hands are grasping your fingers."

The Round Shape

Newborns are developing their eye muscles all the time. According to a compilation of research studies as noted in my book *Baby and Toddler Learning Fun: 50 Interactive and Developmental Activities to Enjoy with Your Child*, babies look here, there, and everywhere, but they prefer a round shape. That certainly fits with how we see them looking at faces. Taking the information one step further, other researchers found that babies prefer round and red to just round. Then somewhere along the line it turned out that round, red, and with a face on it was a baby's favorite.

Materials

Paper plate or red construction paper
Black crayon or nontoxic marker
Scissors
Masking tape or duct tape
Tongue depressor or craft stick

Behind the Scenes

When your baby starts to focus, you can use your puppet for eye-tracking exercises, always moving it in front of your baby from left to right. Because, in English, we learn to read and write in that direction, this specific motion is important from the start.

Research Roundup!

During the first months of life, the eyes start working together and vision rapidly improves, according to the American Optometric Association. Infants will gradually begin tracking moving objects with their eyes. This development also grows babies' eye-hand coordination. The American Academy of Pediatrics recommends that pediatricians examine babies' vision at all well-child visits. These visits can help doctors detect any ocular irregularities, which is an important factor for prompt treatment of any vision issues.

How to Do It

1. Draw a circle with a face on a paper plate or red construction paper with a nontoxic marker or crayon.

2. Using strong masking or duct tape, attach a craft stick or tongue depressor to the back of the paper. The stick will serve as a handle.

3. Hold up your homemade puppet when you want to get your baby's attention.

4. You can also hide the puppet behind your back and then show it to your baby. Repeat this activity for as long as your baby enjoys it.

Looking Up

The first gross motor milestone for a newborn is holding up his head. Therefore, positions and play that stimulate that movement are appropriate.

Materials
Soft pillow

Behind the Scenes
Spending time lying on the tummy is especially important today because babies are often on their backs in different kinds of infant seats. While these carriers provide calming and protection, they limit movement for long periods.

Research Roundup!
According to Robert Pantell, author of *Taking Care of Your Child*, placing your baby on his tummy is a simple thing you can do to help increase upper-back strength. "After you place your baby tummy down on a blanket or play mat on the floor, get down on your own stomach" to play with him. Pantell also recommends that you should "smile, talk, sing, make funny faces, jiggle a set of keys, or put a toy" within his reach.

Engaging your baby will make him more active and, in turn, will build the muscles he will need to roll and eventually crawl. Safe to Sleep, a national education campaign, recommends that babies benefit most from two to three sessions per day of tummy time in three- to five-minute increments.

How to Do It

1. On a soft surface, place your baby on his tummy, facing you. Place a small, soft pillow under your baby's tummy to aid with lifting the chest.

2. Do what comes naturally to attract his attention. He will try to move his head upward. You can also stroke his back to encourage this movement.

3. Once you start to see your baby's head or body move up, show your joy. Your newborn will appreciate every minute of your delight.

4. Continue this kind of play for as long as you and your baby are still having fun.

Who's There?

Once a newborn achieves head control, his back will keep getting stronger until he is finally strong enough to roll over. Therefore, positions that foster back strengthening are beneficial.

Materials
Mirror

Behind the Scenes
A mirror has an important characteristic for your little one: surprise. Mirror images continually change, and your baby will enjoy watching the two of you.

How to Do It

1. Hold your baby with his back against you, and carry him to a convenient wall mirror.

2. Support him with one hand as low as possible on his chest. Place your other hand wherever added support is needed, whether over his knees or under his bottom.

3. Stand in a position so that you and your baby can easily see yourselves in the mirror. Your baby will naturally exercise his back as he leans over to see his reflection. Do not be surprised about gurgles and coos. Those are just some of the many perks for you two as you spend time together.

Research Roundup!

A mirror is described as one of the best toys for baby development by renowned child psychologist Burton White in his landmark book *The First Three Years of Life*. If you plan to use handheld mirrors, Dr. White recommends using only unbreakable types.

Encourage Social-Emotional Growth with Lots of Love

Where Is Baby?

Baby's favorite word is his name. Many songs and rhymes are appropriate, but none are likely to be as interesting and enjoyable as this one with your baby's name in it. A personalized song directly enhances early bonding.

Materials

None

Behind the Scenes

Learning begins at birth, and repetition and familiarity play the biggest roles in your child's development. If you start early with specific songs and actions and keep them going, you will see that those words and your motions will be remembered by you and your baby for years to come.

Research Roundup!

From "Baby Brains: The First Year" by Yudhijit Bhattacharjee in *National Geographic* magazine comes important learning research. "At birth the brain has nearly a hundred billion neurons, as many as in adulthood. As the baby grows, receiving a flood of sensory input, neurons get wired to other

How to Do It

1. With your baby sitting in your lap, clap your baby's hands together to the tune of "Frère Jacques."

2. Follow the simple directions as you sing the words.

   Where is (baby's name)?
   Where is (baby's name)?
   Here I am. (Help baby point to herself)
   Here I am. (Help baby point to herself)
   How are you today, Miss?
   Very well, I thank you.
   Raise your right hand. (Raise baby's right hand)
   Raise your left hand. (Raise baby's left hand)

neurons, resulting in some hundred trillion connections by age three." Different stimuli help establish different neural networks, and circuits get strengthened through repeated activation. Each circuit that gets activated represents learning, and learning on the baby/toddler level is an everyday, all-day-long, rapid-fire process very much influenced by repetition.

Pat-a-Cake

This song, with its simple tune and actions, provides an excellent beginning rhyme. With your newborn, gentle, regular clapping is best.

Materials
None

Behind the Scenes
The secret salsa with this activity is the social interaction it provides. These well-known words make it easy for almost anyone to engage a baby. Eye contact is likely to be fostered by your spontaneous smiles and happy voice. The cross clap, roll, and stir movements also stimulate left-right brain integration. While it is too early now from a motor point of view to do these motions as described with your newborn, it is excellent to know about them for later use.

Research Roundup!
Infants and toddlers need unhurried time with their parents to form critical relationships with them, according to *From Neurons to Neighborhoods: The Science of Early Childhood Development* from the Institute of Medicine. Providing this kind of relaxed environment for little ones creates a positive foundation for social, emotional, and cognitive development,

How to Do It
1. Place your baby in a position so that his hands and arms are free for movement.
2. Say the rhyme to your baby and clap your baby's hands.

Pat-a-cake, pat-a-cake, baker's man. (Clap hands to the beat)
Bake me a cake as fast as you can. (Clap hands)
Roll it (Roll arms one over the other)
And stir it (Move hand around)
And mark it with a (Initial of baby's name) (Trace letter on baby's hand)
And toss it (Toss arms out)
In the oven for (Baby's name) (Point to baby)
And me. (Point to self)

and is optimal for early development. Such a loose structure gives parents the opportunity to know their children better and be able to recognize even the most subtle cues that indicate what children need to promote their healthy growth and development.

If You're Happy and You Know It

This song, with its simple movements, is excellent for creating a happy mood.

How to Do It

1. Place your baby in a position in which his hands and feet are free for movement.

2. Sing this song and do the movements as marked.

If you're happy and you know it, clap your hands. (Clap hands)
If you're happy and you know it, clap your hands. (Clap hands)
If you're happy and you know it, then your face will surely show it.
If you're happy and you know it, clap your hands. (Clap hands)

If you're happy and you know it, stamp your feet. (Gently stamp feet)
If you're happy and you know it, stamp your feet. (Stamp feet)
If you're happy and you know it, then your face will surely show it.
If you're happy and you know it, stamp your feet. (Stamp feet)

If you're happy and you know it, pat your head. (Gently pat head)
If you're happy and you know it, pat your head. (Pat head)
If you're happy and you know it, then your face will surely show it.
If you're happy and you know it, pat your head. (Pat head)

If you're happy and you know it, do all three. (Clap hands, stamp feet, pat head)
If you're happy and you know it, do all three. (Clap hands, stamp feet, pat head)
If you're happy and you know it, then your face will surely show it.
If you're happy and you know it, do all three. (Clap hands, stamp feet, pat head)

Materials

None

Behind the Scenes

Because most everyone likes to be happy, a song about being happy can create that feeling. Using three actions at the end adds to the fun and will also support memory development. Three items in a sequence provide an appropriate memory challenge for young children; two are easy to remember, and four or more are more difficult.

In 1971, Burton White of Harvard University completed thirty years of research on this question: "What is it that is different in the lives of children who succeed in school from those who do not?" He discovered it was all based on positive experiences in the first three years. Children who were well-developed by that time were more likely to be successful in school at age six.

Skida Marink

The words to this song suggest love, which is so important to your growing relationship with your newborn. If you do not know the tune, say the words like you would if you were reciting a poem.

Materials

None

Behind the Scenes

This song provides a loving interaction between parent and baby. The motions lay the groundwork for later, more organized sign language that you might decide to teach.

Research Roundup!

People are inherently social from birth say Valdosta State University psychologists William G. Huitt and Courtney Dawson. They quote theorist John Bowlby, "an infant's attachment to a caregiver serves as the foundation for all future social development." Another theorist, Erik Erikson, says, "an infant will develop trust through interaction with a warm, available, and responsive caregiver." It is vital to form strong attachments in infancy, because, as renowned researcher Mary Ainsworth found, attachment patterns remain "fairly stable" throughout a person's life.

How to Do It

1. Hold your baby in a comfortable position.

2. Bounce your baby as you sing or say the words and follow the simple directions.

   Skida marink a dink a dink.
   Skida marink a do.
   I (Point to self) *love* (Cross arms on yourself) *you.* (Point to baby)

   I love you in the morning
   And in the afternoon.
   I love you in the evening
   And underneath the moon.

   Oh, skida marink a dink a dink
   Skida marink a do.
   I (Point to self) *love* (Cross arms on yourself) *you.* (Point to baby)

Peekaboo

Every parent seems to know one version or another of this social game. Just as with pat-a-cake and "If You're Happy and You Know It," you can begin the interaction with your newborn on a simple level and then work toward more extensive play as your baby grows.

Materials
None

Behind the Scenes
This game is completely interactive. Start by covering and uncovering your eyes with your hands, and then add variations. A little washcloth will soon be great for hiding your or your child's whole face. Turning yourself away comes much later. Eventually, peekaboo will turn into the universal childhood favorite, hide and seek.

Research Roundup!
Dr. Caspar Addyman, researcher at Birkbeck College in London, studies baby laughter and shed some light on peekaboo. Your newborn, of course, does not yet understand object permanence—knowing that an object still exists even if it goes out of sight—but likes peekaboo just for the sheer joy of seeing you appear, disappear, and then quickly appear once again! "Peekaboo is all the best things," says Dr. Addyman. On the beginning level it is just about surprise, and then on the next level it adds the experience of anticipation.

How to Do It

1. Place your baby in a position so that you both can see each other.

2. Cover your eyes with your hands.

3. Remove your hands and say, "Peekaboo."

4. Repeat the activity for as long as you two continue to have fun with it. Your baby will delight in seeing you disappear and then reappear again. The element of surprise is an integral part of the best kinds of play.

Promote Language Learning with Sounds, Rhymes, and Reading

Coo, Gurgle, and Smile Too!

Responding to a newborn's vocalizations with the same sounds encourages your baby to vocalize more. This same principle also works for smiling.

Materials
None

How to Do It

1. Whenever you are with your baby, listen for coos and gurgles.

2. If you hear one, repeat it back.

3. Look for smiles too. Then smile back.

Behind the Scenes

Human speech is interactive. One communication invites another, and many responses elicit answers back. Today, because much language comes from screens and digital devices that cannot provide this kind of personal interaction, time interacting with and responding to children is important.

Research Roundup!

"Although babies do not understand the meaning of words, they do understand tonal nuances and love when your voice sounds admiring, enchanted with them, and happy," says Alice Honig in "Keys to Quality Infant Care: Nurturing Every Baby's Life Journey." Honig stresses the importance of nurturing and communicating with your baby as much as possible.

Soothing Sounds

Soothing sounds such as soft music or a bell encourage a newborn to vocalize. Even just hearing pleasant conversations between you and others will lay the groundwork for your baby to eventually be able to make many sounds.

Materials

Items to make soothing sounds, such as a music box; a bell; glass with a spoon for clinking; two blocks to rub together; a rattle; or a sealed plastic container with paper clips, uncooked rice, or noodles

Behind the Scenes

Pleasant sounds provide a wonderful vehicle for attracting your baby's attention and, as a result, stimulating vocalizations. Such baby sounds are the forerunners of speech and are very important.

How to Do It

1. Collect as many sources of soothing sounds as you can. As you choose objects, never use anything so small that your baby could swallow it.

2. Make a sound and listen for your baby's response.

3. Respond back in your own happy way.

4. Repeat this kind of sequence with all your different sound items and for as long as you and your baby keep enjoying them.

Research Roundup!

"Physical loving" refers to the love a child can experience by being rocked in a rocking chair and snuggling in a carrier, according to Alice Honig. She recommends being gentle as a way to get tender loving responses in return. Try speaking calmly and even dancing cheek-to-cheek to slow waltz music, to grow closeness. She tells us, "A baby responds when you are an attentive and delighted talking partner." Honig refers to the 1971 research of Ashley Montagu who says, "To be tender, loving and caring, human beings must be tenderly loved and cared for in their earliest years."

Nursery Rhymes

Nursery rhymes have been a part of newborn culture for generations. The rhythm, beat, and meaning of the words lay the foundation for future language development.

Materials
None

Behind the Scenes
Repetition plays a big role in the learning process, and it is especially important for babies. Choose one or two rhymes that you like, and have fun saying them at different times and in different places.

Research Roundup!
Researchers from Cambridge University in England showed that babies are attuned to nursery rhymes and that these lyrical pieces provide positive mother-baby interaction that is beneficial to their language development. Research led by Victoria Leong found that nursery rhymes are a good way for mothers to get in sync with their babies. Her team also concluded that babies responded better when there was prolonged eye contact. Mothers who recited nursery rhymes while looking directly at their babies held their babies' attention significantly better than those who gazed away, even occasionally.

How to Do It

1. Think of nursery rhymes that you already know, and have fun saying them to your baby. Some old favorites are "Humpty Dumpty," "Hey Diddle, Diddle," and "Old King Cole."

2. If you know any hand or finger movements for your rhymes, do those too.

3. If your baby babbles at any time during the rhyme, stop and babble back.

Clapping Patterns

Clapping patterns are of interest to newborns. They also stimulate an awareness of sound differentiations.

Materials
None

Behind the Scenes
Both auditory and visual pattern recognition are part of child learning. Clapping patterns help with listening comprehension.

Research Roundup!
According to a study by April Benasich and her fellow researchers at Rutgers University, *acoustic mapping* can boost a baby's auditory system in a way that can help

How to Do It

1. Place your baby in a position in which you can clap both your hands and your baby's hands.

2. Clap short patterns using loud and soft claps.

3. Clap the same ones using your baby's hands.

4. Use the words *loud* and *soft* as you clap, as in "loud, soft, soft," and "loud, loud, soft."

5. Repeat the patterns as often as you and your baby enjoy them.

with speech and language delays. Very early on, an infant makes brain "maps" of the speech sounds of his language. These maps make it easier for the baby to quickly and easily piece together more sounds and then understand them as spoken words. Speech and language is an incredibly complicated process that requires distinguishing auditory patterns only a few milliseconds in length and allows immediate understanding of individual speech sounds such as "bay" and "bee" and then puts them together into words such as *baby*. Early exposure to certain sounds seems to help the brain to more effectively process auditory information by turning them into brain pathways.

Reading Time

Reading to your baby is the finest preparation for your child later learning to read, and it is never too early to start. Rhythm, vocabulary, and feeling all play a role in this activity.

Materials
Children's book

Behind the Scenes
The more you read, sing, and talk to your child, the higher his comprehension level will become. All language fosters comprehension and provides a foundation for later talking, reading, and writing.

Research Roundup!
In my PhD dissertation, I discuss a high correlation between high-quality and -quantity adult-to-child language and child achievement. *High-quality language* has these major components: showing approval through praise, having a pleasant tone, modeling correct grammar, extending child words to complete a phrase, adding new information to child expressions, implementing language that stimulated a response, and using open-ended questions.

How to Do It

1. Select a book with simple pictures and large, clear words. You can use any book, but you will probably prefer those with durable pages. Many are specially made to be read to babies and toddlers. Some also have textures for your baby to touch, and those are highly recommended.

2. Get comfortable, with your baby on your lap. Hold him in a way that you can easily read to him.

3. Talk about the pictures and point to the words as you read them.

Enhance Self-Esteem with Self-Awareness Songs and Rhymes

Head, Shoulders, Knees, and Toes

This song is about four distinct parts of the body. As you shower your attention on your baby for each one, you will see him respond happily.

Materials

None

Behind the Scenes

Paying attention to your baby plays a major role in raising his self-esteem level. By pointing out different parts of your baby's body, you are showing interest in him, and your baby will like that.

Research Roundup!

Spending time with your baby can boost his self-esteem, according to the article "Boost Your Baby's Self-Esteem" by Melissa Balmain. She quotes Neil Boris of the Tulane Institute of Infant and Early Childhood Mental Health in New Orleans, who has researched the concept of attachment. "When an infant promptly gets what she craves like a hug, a bottle, a clean diaper," he says, "she develops a sense of order and predictability that is the foundation of confidence." He describes this process as attachment. His studies suggest that securely attached babies and toddlers are more likely to become confident preschoolers and grade-schoolers. Parents often worry about giving in to crying babies or picking them up too much, but this research shows how important attentiveness is in making a baby feel secure. According to Boris, paying attention to your baby will decrease the need for him to cry out in the first place.

How to Do It

1. Place your baby in a comfortable position in which his hands are free.

2. As you sing or say the words to the following rhyme, point to those parts on your baby.

3. In time, as your baby grows, you two can have the same singing and pointing experience by pointing to your corresponding body parts.

   Head, shoulders, knees, and toes.
   Knees and toes.
   Head, shoulders, knees, and toes.
   Knees and toes.
   And eyes and ears and mouth and nose.
   Head, shoulders, knees, and toes.
   Knees and toes.

Where Is Thumbkin?

This song helps you focus on your newborn's hands and fingers. It is a way of opening up the fingers and introducing finger names.

Materials

None

Behind the Scenes

"Where Is Thumbkin?" is a natural follow-up to "Head, Shoulders, Knees, and Toes" for both memory development and self-awareness. It also helps you put positive attention on your baby's hands in general and fingers in particular.

Research Roundup!

Interacting in a positive way with your baby is very important for boosting your baby's self-esteem, says Zero to Three, an organization dedicated to research about the first three years. While babies may not understand your every word, they know whether your facial expression is approving or not.

How to Do It

1. Place your baby in a comfortable position, making sure that you both can see his hands and fingers.

2. As you sing the song, open up each finger as you name it: thumb, pointer, tall man (middle finger), ring finger, pinky.

   Where is Thumbkin? Where is Thumbkin? (Open baby's thumb)
   Here I am. Here I am. (Touch thumb)
   How are you today, sir?
   Very well, I thank you.
   Run away. Run away. (Gently fold baby's thumb)

3. Repeat the same format with the other fingers.

This Little Piggy Went to Market

This classic rhyme helps you show interest in your newborn's feet. It is also a way of helping your baby to become more aware of having ten individual toes.

How to Do It

1. Place your baby in a comfortable position.

2. As you say each line of the following rhyme to your baby, touch one of the toes on your baby's left foot, going from largest to smallest.

3. When you get to the pinky toe, follow the directions.

4. Repeat the whole process again for your baby's right foot.

   This little piggy went to market. (Touch the big toe)
   This little piggy stayed home. (Touch the second toe)
   This little piggy had roast beef. (Touch the third toe)
   This little piggy had none. (Touch the fourth toe)
   And this little piggy cried, "Wee! Wee! Wee!" all the way home. (Touch the pinky toe and then move your fingers all the way up your baby's body to his chin)

Materials

None

Behind the Scenes

Songs are a great way to enjoy time with your baby.

Research Roundup!

Zero to Three recommends being there as the most important directive for promoting baby self-esteem. "When your baby learns a skill like rolling over or waving bye-bye, cheer him and hug him with abandon," says child-development specialist Stefanie Powers, as quoted in an article by Melissa Balmain. "The more you delight in a baby's activities," she adds, "the more you send a powerful message that he really matters and what he is doing is important."

Hickory Dickory Dock

This rhyme helps you introduce your newborn to the basic beginning concepts of *up*, *down*, and *one*. While using this kind of experiential learning, you and your baby will also have fun.

How to Do It

1. Place your baby in a comfortable position in which you can easily move him up and down.

2. As you say the following rhyme to your baby, move your baby up to the word *up* and down to the word *down*.

   Hickory dickory dock.
   The mouse ran up the clock. (Move baby up)
   The clock struck one.
   The mouse ran down. (Move baby down)
   Hickory dickory dock.

3. Repeat the rhyme again, but this time leave your baby seated on your lap. Position him comfortably so that he can see you do the actions this way:

   Hickory dickory dock.
   The mouse ran up the clock. (Wiggle your fingers and move your hand up)
   The clock struck one. (Show one finger)
   The mouse ran down. (Wiggle your fingers and move your hand down)
   Hickory dickory dock.

4. If all is going well, do the whole sequence again.

Materials
None

Behind the Scenes
Moving baby up and down to feel these concepts in a happy way directly affects the emergence of self-esteem and language development.

Research Roundup!
Maybe you have seen a smile already and maybe not. In an article by Maureen Connolly, "Your Baby: 10 Milestones for the First 2 Years," your baby will start to exhibit social smiles around three months of age. "A social smile is reciprocal, meaning your baby smiles in response to someone else's smile. It's a sign that several different parts of the brain are maturing." Even just the sound of your voice or the sight of your face is often all it will take to trigger a grin.

Little Boy Blue

This rhyme helps you introduce another body-awareness concept to your newborn: *under.* It also focuses, in a pleasant way, on the process of sleep.

Materials

Blanket

Behind the Scenes

Because *under* and *sleep* are two concepts that are also related to body awareness, this rhyme can help make them enjoyable, too. Because you put your baby under his covers at night or for a nap, and because the main focus of the rhyme is on sleep, enjoy this rhyme with your baby at bedtime or nap time.

Research Roundup!

Self-esteem manifests at different stages, and newborns do not have it because they do not see themselves as being separate from their parents. Lay the groundwork for it by interacting with your baby gently, responding when he cries, and giving lots of cuddles and smiles. In "Simple Ways to Build Your Baby's Self-Esteem," an article in *Psychology Today*, parenting expert Meri Wallace says that parents should do the following to build baby's self-esteem:

- Smile at your baby as much as possible.

- Spend time with him.

- Repeatedly praise your baby and his accomplishments.

- Choose your words carefully when you are communicating. Always try to speak in a positive way to your baby.

How to Do It

1. Place your baby in a comfortable position in which he can have direct eye contact with you.

2. As you say the following rhyme to your baby and come to the word *under,* communicate that concept by putting a blanket over your baby.

3. If it happens also to be bedtime or nap time, you can put your baby under the blanket and then emphasize the word *sleep* with your hands next to your cheek.

Little boy blue,
Come blow your horn.
The sheep's in the meadow.
The cow's in the corn.
But where is the boy who
*   looks after the sheep?*
He's under (Snuggle your
   baby under a baby blanket)
The haystack fast asleep.
   (Pretend to sleep, with
   your hands next to your
   cheek)

2 Three to Six Months

The general responses you observed in the first three months are becoming more refined. As you read, sing, and talk to your baby, you will enjoy seeing beginning reactions of understanding. If something falls, your baby will notice it. Perceptions of loud, soft, big, small, near, far, and many other concepts will become part of your baby's world. Home will start to become familiar. No longer satisfied with what you show your child, she will begin the lifelong journey of exploration as she seeks information for herself.

Your little one will start touching anything she can get her hands on and then put most of that in her mouth. You know what that means: Be very careful with what is available, and be sure it is clean and not small enough to be swallowed. Smile as your baby begins to imitate what you do and even make some of the same sounds. What fun it is to see your baby reach out and grasp for objects. It is even more fun to see her watch people and things as they move from her field of sight.

Develop Skills with More Activities

Continue working with your baby through the activities as before. Go in order or choose an area you want to explore further. You can also look over the following milestones of development for guidance.

Milestones of Development

- Watches her own fingers and hands
- Explores things by putting them in her mouth
- Is attracted to people more than objects
- Responds to a sound that is out of sight
- Reaches and grasps for an object
- Uses objects to make noise
- Searches for a partially hidden object
- Anticipates reappearance of an object
- Grasps two objects at the same time
- Visually follows a fallen object
- Imitates a vocal sound
- Looks, reaches, and grasps at the same time

- Sits with support
- Rolls from back to stomach
- Shows pleasure
- Imitates social interaction
- Uses gestures to show likes and dislikes
- Responds to changes in speech with vocalizations
- Responds to facial expressions with vocalizations
- Recognizes familiar objects by name
- Recognizes people by name
- Babbles vowels and consonant sounds
- Imitates sounds
- Vocalizes to toys and mirror image

Expand Cognitive Skills with Daily Play

Surprise

A focus on any or all of the five senses (sight, sound, taste, touch, and smell) creates learning. Because your baby sees you and specific objects around you almost all the time, she will follow you and those objects with her eyes until you move or the object moves out of sight.

Materials
Safe and appealing items, such as a small paper cup, a plastic spoon, a small box, a rattle, or a small ball
Washcloth

Behind the Scenes
Surprise is one of the four basic elements of high-quality play. No matter the age, surprise can be enjoyable. With sight being the focus here, this more advanced version of peekaboo should be a big hit.

How to Do It

1. Collect some interesting objects. Always check that items are too big to be swallowed.

2. Put the washcloth over each item, one at a time. When you cover an item, say something like, "Where is the ball?"

3. When you remove the cloth, respond with, "Here it is!"

Research Roundup!

InfantSEE® is a public health program of the American Optometric Association (AOA) Foundation. It is designed to ensure that eye and vision care become integral parts of infant wellness for all babies, regardless of a family's income or access to insurance coverage. According to the organization's website, "Eye and vision problems in infants can cause developmental delays. It is important to detect any problems early to ensure babies have the opportunity to develop the visual abilities they need to grow and learn." Under this program, AOA optometrists provide a no-cost comprehensive eye and vision assessment for infants anytime during the first year of life. To learn more about the program, visit www.AOAFoundation.org/infantsee/

Mirror Fun

Creativity is at the heart of this game. Each time you look in the mirror with your baby, you will probably think of something new and different to do or say.

Materials

Wall mirror or handheld mirror

Behind the Scenes

A mirror can provide endless fun. It captures a variety of ongoing, interactive facial and language experiences. Because you two will never see the same images or react the same way twice, there will be no limit to the actions and sounds you could both end up creating.

Research Roundup!

According to Penelope Leach in her book *Your Baby & Child: From Birth to Age Five*, "play is much more than 'just fun' to babies." It is also a time for babies to learn what they can do. Babies will be practicing doing things, finding out about what is around them, and exploring surroundings. She explains that while play might sound specific, a "baby can get some play value out of every single ordinary, pleasant happening in her day".

How to Do It

1. Take your baby to a convenient mirror. Be sure you are both in a comfortable position.

2. Ask, "Who is that?" and "What is that?"

3. Embellish the activity with actions that will encourage more language and more sounds back to you. For example, you might want to nod your head, make a clucking sound, tap your feet, clap your hands, or do something else silly or fun. You two will probably keep giving each other new and wonderful ideas.

See It! Touch It! Now Taste!

Because you will probably see mouthing a lot, cleanliness is key. Make sure that your baby is exploring safe items, with no sharp edges, and nothing small enough to be swallowed. When you are prepared, happy play can continue.

Materials

Objects to explore, such as smooth wooden clothespin (type without a spring), brightly colored hair scrunchie, rattle, plastic spoon, small plastic cup, thick piece of ribbon (8–12 inches long)

Behind the Scenes

The five senses are avenues for learning, and the more of them that can be used at one time, the stronger and more valuable the play experience. With this simple exploratory activity, you can enhance play greatly by using abundant language.

Research Roundup!

According to guidance from the American Association of Pediatrics, teething is likely to start when your baby gets close to six months. The two front teeth (central incisors), either upper or lower, usually appear first, followed by the opposite front teeth. Look for the first molars after that, and then the canines or eyeteeth should appear, though there is great variability in the timing of teething. If your baby does not show any teeth until after this period, that is fine. The timing may be determined by heredity, and it does not mean that anything is wrong. It makes sense that because of the possible discomfort associated with teething, mouthing—both with small toys and objects—seems to coincide with the slow and steady growth of new teeth.

How to Do It

1. Put out some interesting objects for your baby to explore. **Safety note: Do not leave your baby unattended with these items.**

2. As your baby picks up and plays with the items, make sure to name and describe them.

3. Mention characteristics such as color, texture, uses, and any other ideas that you may have.

4. As you name each item and give its description, you are enriching the basic mouthing experience by incorporating the sense of sound and language development.

Pull It In

Your baby will begin to reach for, grasp, and then drop almost anything in sight. While you may often want to discourage this process, now is the time to enjoy and encourage it.

Materials

18" rope, ribbon, or yarn
An item to attach rope to, such as a paper or plastic cup, plastic spoon, child's large bead, small stuffed animal, or plaything that you might have that is appealing and safe

Behind the Scenes

Reaching out, grasping, and then dropping items is a natural part of development. By adding surprise to this concept, you will end up with an excellent opportunity for optimal play.

Research Roundup!

Eye-hand coordination is now developing, and your baby is beginning to notice things she would like to hold. "By three months," as reported on Psychology.jrank.org, "most infants will have made an important hand-eye connection; they can deliberately bring their hands into their field of vision." Babies at this stage will also swipe at things in their view, "a repetitive activity that provides practice in estimating distance and controlling the hands."

Funny Fingers

Use an old glove for this activity. Once the play is over, wash out the glove to use it the next time.

Materials
An old glove
Nontoxic scents to spray, such as lemon or lime juice or vinegar

Behind the Scenes
Because it is difficult to provide natural smell experiences for little ones, this easy-to-play game can provide your baby that exposure. There are many toys available with smells from chemicals, but these are not safe for babies and not recommended.

Research Roundup!
According to Penelope Leach, "As soon as a baby comes out of the womb, all his senses are bombarded with stimuli, and learning through the senses goes on from that moment." She explains that babies react to bad or good smells similarly to adults, turning away from ones they don't like and staying with those that are pleasant. She even goes so far as to say that in some ways "their ability to differentiate between one smell and another far surpasses ours."

Practice Motor Skills with a Focus On Movement

Pull-Ups

This is a pull-to-sit activity. Eventually it will work into a pull-to-stand position.

Materials
None

Behind the Scenes
Because opportunities for exercise and moving are often limited, having a fun and personalized strength-building pull-up game, complete with positive attention, is excellent for all-around muscle development.

How to Do It

1. Have your baby lie down on a soft carpet or bed.

2. As she grasps your hands, slowly pull her up to a sitting position. Gently lay your baby back down and begin again.

3. Keep this activity going in a loving way for as long as you both keep enjoying it.

Research Roundup!
Penelope Leach, in her book *Your Baby & Child: From Birth to Age Five,* explains that once you give your baby your hands, she will love to pull up. Back strength is the key, and as your baby's back gets stronger, your pull can get weaker. That is the fun part for you, experiencing less exertion while your baby enjoys more independent movement.

Tummy Time Together

Many parents today know about the value of making time to put a baby on her tummy. While not a favorite for a baby, there are ways to make it more fun.

Materials
Blanket

Behind the Scenes
Tummy time is a relatively new term in the world of baby play, and it is very important for your baby's motor development. It means consciously providing a time for your baby to be on her tummy and move as much as possible in this position. The more your baby uses muscles while in this position, the stronger those muscles will become.

How to Do It

1. On a blanket or soft floor, lie down on your stomachs opposite each other.

2. Let your fingertips be close to each other but not touching.

3. While stretching out to try to touch each other's hands, encourage your baby to stretch her hands toward yours. You will probably both end up smiling and laughing as you reach out toward each other.

Research Roundup!
According to the American Pediatric Association, children develop motor skills from the head down. Typically, children who are behind in developmental

milestones catch up with other children. The AAP has developed a milestone checklist for parents and caregivers to ensure that children are progressing typically. Visit https://www.healthychildren.org/English/MotorDelay/Pages/default.aspx for more information.

Kick Your Feet

When your baby is on her back, you will notice kicking. Using a beach ball, you can stimulate those movements even more.

Materials
12" beach ball

Behind the Scenes
Movements of all kind are important for development, and kicking and balancing are part of the fun. A small beach ball has just the right colors, size, and texture to stimulate kicking and promote balance.

<table>
<tr><td>

How to Do It

1. Place your baby on her back on a bed or other soft, safe spot.

2. Hold the ball over her head and watch for kicking.

3. Gently move the ball to your baby's feet and assist her in balancing it.

</td></tr>
</table>

Research Roundup!
From three to six months is the time when the baby "will discover and begin to play with his feet," according to *The New First Three Years of Life* by Burton White. This is also the time you will see beginning vigorous arm and leg activity. As with all motor accomplishments, your baby will enjoy practicing these movements. Therefore, as part of what might look to you like your baby's sheer delight with life, this joyful kicking is likely to please you as well.

Biking through Town

It is great fun for your baby when you move her feet in a bicycle movement. This cross-pattern exercise prepares your child for crawling, walking, and eventually running.

Materials
None

Behind the Scenes
Parents often take for granted that little ones will be crawling and walking without any intervention. However, each stage of development is dependent on preparation. Crawling comes after your baby starts rolling over and then sitting up, so this is the right time to do these bicycle leg movements.

Research Roundup!

"Human beings are mobile, and this inborn drive is evident at birth. Therefore, providing an environment all through the early years that is conducive to motor development is important," I say in my book, *Constructive Parenting*. While that, at first, might seem like a daunting task, it turns out that most normal baby and child care opportunities inherently provide these situations. Almost all contact with a little one involves moving, touching, and holding. Each new accomplishment lays the groundwork for the next, and many movements specifically strengthen body muscles. All motor activities in general contribute directly to brain growth and the organization of the nervous system.

With crawling being such a major milestone that is dependent on both back and leg strength, it is natural for parents to focus on leg movements.

How to Do It

1. Find a soft, safe spot and gently lay your baby down.

2. Hold your baby's calves right under her knees.

3. Gently move your baby's legs in a bicycle motion to the tune of "Daisy, Daisy." Here are the words:

   *Daisy, Daisy, give me your
       answer, do.
   I'm half crazy all for the love
       of you.
   It won't be a stylish marriage.
   I can't afford a carriage.
   But you'll look sweet upon
       the seat
   Of a bicycle built for two.*

The Magic Carpet

Movement begets movement. Moving your baby, even on a blanket, stimulates motion.

Materials
Blanket

Behind the Scenes
All through early childhood, children are happiest when they are in motion. Movement is also vital to brain growth and learning.

How to Do It

1. Place your baby on a small blanket.

2. Slowly move the blanket, with her on it, in any direction.

3. Make eye contact with your baby as you move her, and encourage her movement.

Research Roundup!

"Movement is important from the beginning of life," according to Janet Gonzalez-Mena in "What To Do for a Fussy Baby: A Problem-Solving Approach." Allowing a baby to move her limbs, particularly if she is fussy, will help her feel independent and may calm her. Even for the smallest infants, "Movement is not just about exercise and motor development, it's about learning as well as social-emotional and cognitive development."

Encourage Social-Emotional Growth with Loving Communication

Texture and Sound

Many different kinds of household items can be turned into play items, and small plastic baggies work great for learning about textures and sound.

Materials

Snack or sandwich-size plastic baggies
Nontoxic substance such as salt, sugar, rice, dry beans, cornmeal, breadcrumbs, oats, or dry cereal
Packing tape

Behind the Scenes

People are social beings, meant to interact with each other. As you continue to participate in the social-development process with your baby, these small texture and sound bags will provide your baby with many ways to express herself.

Research Roundup!

Three-month-old babies love to touch and mouth objects, according to Renate Zangl, author of *Raising a Talker*. She recommends saying the name of an item while your baby explores it. This practice will help grow your baby's memory of words.

Imitating

Learning to imitate plays a major role in social development, and responding with the same sound is a great way to foster that skill. When your baby makes a sound, imitate that sound for her.

Materials

None

Behind the Scenes

Imitation is an important stage of development, and it plays a big role in the social arena. Begin by imitating your baby, and she will learn to respond to you.

How to Do It

1. Fill a few baggies, each with a different substance.

2. Put each filled baggie into another baggie.

3. Seal the bags tightly with tape. **Safety note: Never leave your baby unattended with a plastic bag.**

4. Have fun together as you squeeze the different baggies, enjoying the textures and sounds.

1. Sit with your baby in a comfortable spot, such as a bed or favorite chair. You might want to keep your baby on your lap. In whatever position you choose, make sure you maintain eye contact.

2. When your baby makes a noise, repeat the noise back to her.

3. Make a gurgle, coo, or babble and wait for your baby's response. You can even clap your hands to try to get a response. Do what comes naturally, and then repeat anything and everything your baby says.

Research Roundup!

From the book *Caring for Your Baby and Young Child: Birth to Age 5,* we learn that three to six months is the time for babbling. "Although it may sound like gibberish, if you listen closely, you'll hear her raise and drop her voice as if she is making a statement or asking a question." You can encourage this kind of communication by talking to your baby a lot. "When she says a recognizable syllable, repeat it back to her and then say some simple words that contain that sound." Here are some choices: "box, bonnet," and "baa, baa, black sheep."

Up, Up, and Around

You can play this fun game lying on a bed, sitting in a chair, or standing.

Materials

None

Behind the Scenes

While movement is the focus in this activity, making eye contact is the key for social development. As you move your baby, you stay connected both physically and mentally, and that fosters your developing personal relationship.

Research Roundup!

"Making eye contact is the most powerful mode of establishing a communicative link between humans. During their first year of life, infants learn rapidly that the looking behaviors of others conveys significant information," according to "Eye Contact Detection in Humans From Birth," a 2002 study published in the *Proceedings of the National*

How to Do It

1. Keep close eye contact with your baby and begin to gently move her in different directions, such as up, down, and around, and gently bounce her on your lap.

2. **Always hold on to your baby**. It is not secure for her to be disconnected from you in any way at any time, even for a few seconds.

3. Do what comes naturally as you connect with your little one. Keep playing as long as she is enjoying the movements.

Academy of Sciences on newborns and four-month-olds. Results showed that "from birth, human infants prefer to look at faces when accompanied by direct eye gazes." The sensitivity attained in these two studies pointed to mutual gaze as the major foundation for the later development of social skills.

Give and Take

Your baby is learning to hold on and release. This is a great time to pass items back and forth to each other.

Materials
Safe objects to handle, such as empty salt and pepper shakers, small wrapped decorator soaps, plastic spoons, small paper or plastic cups, plastic toy cars, small dolls, rattles, children's blocks, and other small toys or household items

Behind the Scenes
As with the other activities in this section, this one focuses on back-and-forth interpersonal communication. While most toys are designed for specific play, household items can be used or combined to foster fun and interaction.

Research Roundup!
According to the American Academy of Pediatrics in *Caring for Your Baby and Young Child: Birth to Age 5*, this is the time your baby is likely to evidence a dramatic change in personality. Leaving a time just filled with mostly eating, sleeping, and affection, she is likely to become more attentive to the outside world. While your baby will get bored quickly with even the most engaging toy, she will never tire of what you find and allow her to explore while giving her your undivided attention. "If you run out of the usual toys or she loses interest in them, plastic or wooden spoons, unbreakable cups and jars, or bowl lids and boxes are endlessly entertaining and inexpensive."

How to Do It

1. Place several safe, easy-to-handle, and interesting objects for your baby to observe and touch. **Safety note: Check to be sure that your child cannot swallow the items.**

2. Give your baby one of the items.

3. Put out your hand and ask your baby to give it back to you.

4. Continue play with all the items you have chosen.

5. See if your baby can initiate the giving process.

Getting to Know You

Your baby's favorite place is sitting happily snuggled in your arms. Take advantage of this desire.

Materials
None

Behind the Scenes
During this stage of natural learning, you will continue to build your closeness. Your baby will love getting to know you, and you will enjoy helping her learn about her own features.

Research Roundup!
"Keys to Quality Infant/Toddler Care: Nurturing Baby's Life Journey" by Alice Honig has information about the need and appropriateness of this kind of parent exploration. She explains that it is perfectly normal for some babies to get rough with it and even hurt the parent in the process. Therefore, she cautions to be prepared and know what to do. If your baby "pinches your neck, licks your salty arm, pulls your hair, tugs at your glasses, or shows you in other ways how powerfully important your body is as a sacred and special playground," gently stop her right away. The parent's job is to teach gentleness by calmly describing and showing proper loving actions. In addition, added hugging, kissing, and caressing provide secure comfort.

> ## How to Do It
>
> 1. Place your baby on your lap.
> 2. Watch as she explores your body and face.
> 3. Each time your baby reaches out to you, name the part she touches. Always caution your baby to be gentle.
> 4. Use your baby's hand to point out the corresponding parts on her body and face.

Promote Language Learning with Words, Songs, Rhymes, and Sounds

You Name It

While your baby is busy exploring everyday objects, make sure to name them and talk about characteristics for her. The more words you model for your baby, the better her language development will be.

> ## How to Do It
>
> 1. Take your baby on a field trip around your house.
> 2. Point out interesting items, such as pictures, flowers, candles, the toaster or toaster oven, the coffeemaker, the refrigerator, doors, closets, dressers, and so on.
> 3. Include whatever catches your baby's attention. If a particular object seems to be of special interest, describe it to her.

Fun Baby Learning Games

Materials

None

Behind the Scenes

A rich language environment is of utmost importance to your baby's development. A mix of high-quality words combined with much basic speech is exactly what your baby needs for language growth and learning.

Research Roundup!

According to the American Academy of Pediatrics' *Caring for Your Baby and Young Child: Birth to Age 5*, babies learn language in three stages. From birth it starts from hearing people make sounds. At this time, they listen for pitch and tone to understand meaning. During this three- to six-month-old stage, babies begin noticing not only the way people talk but also what individual sounds they hear. Your baby will "listen to the vowels and consonants and begin to notice the way these combine into syllables, words, and sentences."

Song Time

Singing is a natural way of interacting with your baby. Singing well is not important. Singing what you like and in your own loving way is what matters.

Materials

None

Behind the Scenes

The rhythm and rhyme connected with simple songs enhance learning power. While all words from spoken language can make a positive impact, those that are part of a catchy song are easier to remember.

How to Do It

1. Choose a favorite childhood song of yours and sing it to your baby.

2. Pick more than one, if you wish.

3. Sing any time, any place, and as often as you want.

Research Roundup!

Singing to a baby helps her mood and also enhances the emotional bond to a caregiver, according to the *Psychology Today* article, "Does Singing to Your Baby Really Work?" by Kimberly Sena Moore, PhD. The best part for a parent is to know that your baby does not care about the quality of the singing. Moore reassures parents by saying, "Your baby loves your voice and feels connected to your way of singing," regardless of how it sounds.

Rhyming Fun

Rhymes provide another wonderful way of interacting with your baby. Every culture has its favorites. Try a favorite rhyme you know, or make one up. As with singing, pick a rhyme you enjoy, and your child's language development will follow.

Behind the Scenes

Nursery rhymes have stood the test of time, and they often deliver specific messages or are designed to provide an important lesson. Making up your own poems can provide fun and learning, too.

Research Roundup!

"Phonological awareness in an important precursor in learning to read," according to Laurie J. Harper, in "Nursery Rhyme Knowledge and Phonological Awareness in Preschool Children." "This awareness of phonemes, [the distinct units of sound in a word], fosters a child's ability to hear and blend sounds, encode and decode words, and to spell phonetically." The research supports the idea "that sensitivity to rhyme and alliteration prior to a child's entry to formal schooling plays a causal role in their reading success several years later."

How to Do It

1. Choose one of your favorite childhood rhymes, such as "Little Miss Muffet" or "Little Boy Blue," and say it to your baby.

2. As with songs, choose more than one, if you like.

3. Say them any time, any place, and as often as you want. Repetition is best for your baby's developing mind.

4. To learn more rhymes, visit the library, your local bookstore, or look online.

5. Remember, spur-of-the-moment creativity is always welcome, such as this short rhyme:

   Where are you? I see you.
   There you are. In the car.

Reading Time II

This is a great time to set up a reading routine. Your baby should be able to sit in your lap and give you the sense that she is paying attention. Board books with large, clear words, simple sentences, and pictures are appropriate to read to her.

Materials

Books of your choice

Behind the Scenes

A regular reading time provides a consistent opportunity to engage your child with a rich language environment and added vocabulary. You will also be helping your baby make the connection between speech, printed words, and pictures.

How to Do It

1. Place your baby comfortably on your lap.

2. Read the book to your baby in such a way that you are communicating. Make sure to use eye contact and respond to your baby's babbling.

3. Read her favorite books over and over and keep choosing new ones to expand her learning.

There is sound evidence for read-aloud benefits, according to "Reading Aloud with Infants: The Controversy, the Myth, and a Case Study" by Jeanne W. Holland. Results from Holland's study show that "parents and caregivers reading aloud to infants is necessary in developing literacy skills." Benefits include print awareness, vocabulary development, fluency, and comprehension.

Animal Sounds

Paying attention to animal sounds is part of the language-development process. Mimicking them is delightful and provides listening and speaking practice.

Materials

Magazine or other materials with animal photos, such as zoo photos or children's books

Behind the Scenes

Listening and speaking start the language-development process, and reading and writing form the next two parts of literacy. Your baby picks up language by listening to what people say.

Research Roundup!

"The opportunity to learn from complex stimuli and events are vital early in life, and that success in school begins in infancy," according to Patricia Kuhl, a researcher at the University of Washington. Her highly regarded research suggests children learn more and earlier than previously thought. In another article, Kuhl and her colleagues found that babies are "language universalists" who are able to learn any sound in any language.

How to Do It

1. Find photos of animals and talk about the animals. Use repetitive phrases such as these:

   "What does the duck say? The duck says, 'Quack! Quack!'"
   "What does the dog say? The dog says, 'Bow-wow!'"
   "What does the cat say? The cat says, 'Meow.'"
   "What does the bird say? The bird says, 'Tweet, tweet.'"

2. Listen for ways your baby may try to imitate the different sounds.

Enhance Self-Esteem with Baby's Name, Family Awareness, and Body Movement

Where Is Ethan?

Your baby loves to hear his name, so say it often. Playing a game with your baby's name will make him feel special.

Materials
8 to 10 5" x 8" index cards
Crayon or nontoxic marker

Behind the Scenes
When you keep repeating your child's name, you clearly show that he is valued, needed, and important. Therefore, use his name as much as possible.

Research Roundup!
"Self-esteem is your child's passport to a lifetime of mental health and social happiness. It is the foundation of a child's well-being and the key to success as an adult," according to "12 Ways to Raise a Confident Child" on askdrsears.com. "Addressing your child by name, especially by using eye contact and touch, exudes a 'you're special' message. Beginning an interaction by using the other person's name opens doors, breaks barriers, and even softens corrective discipline. Children learn to associate how you use their name with the message you have and the behavior you expect." What Dr. Sears presents goes beyond theory. He has also noticed that "children with self-confidence more frequently address their peers and adults by name or title. Their own self-worth allows them to be more direct in their communication with others."

How to Do It

1. Write your baby's name on each index card.

2. Place the cards in different places around the room.

3. After they are all placed, collect them with your baby.

4. Each time you pick up a card, say, "Ethan, I found you," or "Ethan, I see you."

5. Have fun making up your own little sayings as you play.

So Big

For this game, when you say the words *so big*, you will raise your baby's arms with pride. Your baby will gradually learn to raise his own arms at the right time.

Behind the Scenes
Games and activities that have been passed down through the generations are wonderful for their familiarity and worthy of your time and attention for the learning they can inspire. The words and actions of So Big, especially with your baby's name used, can inspire self-pride in your baby.

How to Do It

1. Place your baby comfortably in your lap and hold her hands.

2. As you hold hands, ask your baby: "How big is baby?" To make the play more personal and effective, use your child's name.

3. Raise your baby's arms over her head and say, "So-o-o big!" Repeat your play over and over until you feel that you have both had enough.

Research Roundup!

On the Dr. Sears website, "12 Ways to Raise a Confident Child" suggests that parents and other caregivers should practice the carry-over principle. A natural beginning on the baby level is to point out in a proud and joyful way what you notice about the growth of your little one. Dr. Sears's guidance is not to worry about discovering real talent and to just keep pointing out small tasks well done. Here is his key, the carry-over principle: "Enjoying one activity boosts a child's self-image, and this carries over into other endeavors."

Baby's Name Toy

Homemade toys have a special kind of appeal for your baby's learning.

Materials

5" x 8" index cards
Crayon or nontoxic marker
Double-stick tape or glue
Clear contact paper or laminate

Behind the Scenes

With this activity, you are able to expand your baby's recognition of her name in two ways—by visualizing it from her photo and by identifying it in written form. This practice will help lay the groundwork for later reading.

Research Roundup!

Although a baby is able to see at birth, total visual ability takes months to develop, according to *Your Baby & Child: From Birth to Age Five* by Penelope Leach. During this three- to six-months-old stage, your baby can distinguish subtle shades of reds, blues, and yellows. Most babies also enjoy

How to Do It

1. Paste your baby's photograph on an index card.

2. On the other card, write your baby's whole name in large, clear letters.

3. Tape the two cards together back to back so that one side shows your baby's picture and the other her name.

4. Cover the cards with contact paper or laminate them.

5. Point to your baby's name and say it to her.

6. Point to the picture and say her name again.

7. Continue the activity as long as you both enjoy it.

seeing increasingly complex patterns and shapes. "By four months, your baby's range of vision has increased to several feet or more, and it will continue to expand until, at about seven months, her eyesight will be more nearly mature."

Looking at Photos

Your baby will love to look at photos of herself, you, your family, and close friends. Choose whatever viewing medium works best for you—computer, tablet, smartphone, or even a small photo album.

Materials
Family photos

Behind the Scenes
The progression continues. First you exposed your baby to the joy of responding to her name and picture; now you are expanding this recognition to family members and close friends. Seeing and hearing about family and friends in positive ways will help your baby understand that she has a valued place in this social circle.

How to Do It

1. Look at family photos together. Point out the people and name them.

2. If time and interest permit, explain what is going on in each picture. Be sure to hold the device or album at all times so that your baby cannot damage it in any way.

Research Roundup!
With so much focus on parent-child interaction, it is important to keep in mind the importance of a strong and positive family unit. "Building Strong Families—Kids and Self-Esteem" from the University of Missouri's Extension service explains that a strong family unit has protective factors that safeguard children. "Children need to feel safe, secure, loved, and part of a family," in whatever form the family takes.

Hands and Feet

Hair scrunchies are great for this movement activity.

Materials

Hair scrunchies of various colors

Behind the Scenes

Your baby is gaining more control over her hands and feet. By wearing these colorful markers, your little one will be drawn to giving more time and attention to her hand and feet movements.

Research Roundup!

According to the American Academy of Pediatrics' *Caring for Your Baby and Young Child: Birth to Age 5*, physical coordination improves quite a lot from three to six months of age. It will likely seem that your baby is discovering "parts of her body that she never knew existed." When lying on her back, "She can now grab her feet and toes and bring them to her mouth." In time she will "place her newly found feet on the floor . . . curl her toes and stroke the carpet or wood floor surface." This is also the time you are likely to see your baby use both hands together to accomplish a task. With grasping on the way, all the swipes at objects are part of the motor-development process.

How to Do It

1. Place your baby in a safe and comfortable position—on a bed, carpet, or sofa.

2. Place a different color scrunchie on your baby's wrists and ankles. Don't wrap the scrunchies too tight and keep a close watch on her during this play.

3. Watch her move her hands and feet to enjoy the colors and/or sounds.

3 Six to Nine Months

Your baby's skills are growing in every area of development, and he can now engage more with his environment. As he learns to clap hands, manipulate objects, and reach for items, you can see the beginnings of initiating interactions with other people. Responding to your baby is the key. The more you react to your baby's actions and communications, the more he will be encouraged.

Another characteristic that appears at this time is the emergence of uniqueness. Your baby will get a glimpse of seeing himself as an individual. This new perspective will also allow him to experience family identity, which will lead to a sense of security and an appropriate corresponding uneasiness with strangers. Try to be as sensitive as you can to this new awareness.

Activity Time Continues with More Purposeful Play

All your positive responses, great or small, will mean the world to your baby. Keep them coming. As you look over the following developmental milestones, try any or all of the suggested activities. While your baby will value each response you offer, these guided specifics should enhance your time together.

Milestones of Development

- Begins to develop concepts like *in and out* and *up and down*
- Begins pointing
- Performs action to get a result
- Uncovers a hidden object
- Puts objects into a container
- Puts down one object to reach for another
- Transfers object from one hand to the other
- Creeps forward or backward
- Pulls to standing
- Sits unsupported and reaches
- Brings hands together to body at the midline
- Uses pincer grasp (thumb and forefinger)
- Hands object to another person
- Crawls
- Reacts appropriately to strangers
- Responds playfully to a mirror
- Plays Peekaboo
- Shows preferences for people, objects, and places
- Responds to rhythm and vocalizations
- Makes word-like sounds
- Says *dada* and *mama* as sounds
- Vocalizes playfully when left alone
- Enjoys simple songs and rhymes

Enjoy Cognitive Growth by Focusing on Baby Initiative

The Recycle Bin

Just as your recycling materials will change from week to week, so will this game. When you take out items for play, limit your selection to plastic and foam materials. Eliminate cans, glass, plastic with sharp corners or that is cut, and other items that could be dangerous to your baby.

Materials
Plastic and foam materials

Behind the Scenes
With *in and out* and *up and down* being major concepts occurring at this developmental stage, these recyclable materials are tailor-made for that kind of talk. Because plastic containers are of interest at this time, recyclables of all sizes, shapes, and colors should delight your little one. They all lend themselves to descriptive language.

How to Do It

1. Watch your baby select items.

2. See what he puts back.

3. As your child chooses objects, talk about what he is doing with each item, and describe the materials in as much detail as you can.

4. Let the play evolve between the two of you.

5. Help your baby make stacks of the objects and open and shut any covered containers.

Research Roundup!

Infants in the six- to nine-month-old age range can understand the meaning of many spoken words, according to researchers Daniel Swingley and Elika Bergelson in the *Proceedings of the National Academy of Sciences*. Before, the commonly accepted idea was that they began "learning their native language by discovering features of the speech signal: consonants, vowels, and combinations of these sounds." This new information shows evidence that "infants already know the meanings of several common words from the age of six months onward." What is especially interesting is that this study does not negate the first theory. On the contrary, it suggests that learning vocabulary and learning the sound structure of spoken language go hand in hand as language acquisition begins.

Pick One

Your baby loves exerting more control over his environment, and this activity is designed for that purpose.

Materials
Several toys

Behind the Scenes
Your baby now knows how to show preference, and this activity allows him the opportunity to use that skill. You might notice your baby expresses desire by pointing or by making some kind of sound. No matter how he communicates his desire, responding appropriately will fill your baby with joy.

Research Roundup!
An article by Michelle Roberts on the BBC News website points to growing research that shows that babies as young as four months show a preference for certain colors. Dr. Anna Franklin from the Surrey Baby Lab in the United Kingdom has studied more than 250 babies to look at which colors they prefer. She professes that babies are not color-blind at birth and explains that some babies show a striking preference for just one color. When colors were shown to babies in pairs, they tended to look for the longest amount of time at blue, red, purple, and orange and the shortest amount of time at brown. Dr. Franklin has found that babies are also less likely to look at brown first when paired with the other colors, suggesting this is their least-favorite color.

> ### How to Do It
>
> 1. Place two of your baby's toys just out of his reach.
> 2. Notice how he communicates which one he wants. It could be by sound, gesture, or both.
> 3. Give your baby the item of his choice.
> 4. After your baby is finished playing with the toy, set up two other toys.
> 5. Repeat the process.
> 6. Continue playing with different toys until you both have had enough.

Dropping and Throwing

Your baby's new dropping and throwing skills can keep you busy. With this activity, you can turn this play into a game that you will both enjoy.

Materials

Ribbon, yarn, string, or long shoelaces
Toys
Stroller or high chair

Behind the Scenes

The best extension of this activity is at eating time. While you are using your baby spoon to do the feeding, you might want to give your baby another one to hold and experience in his own way. If that is the case, attaching it to his high chair will provide entertainment for your baby as well as cleanliness for you. Once it is secured by an appropriate string or ribbon of choice, you can continue using your spoon and let your baby pitch in too when you help him from time to time.

Research Roundup!

From *The New First Three Years of Life* by Burton White, we learn that baby is gradually shifting the focus of his interest from motor skills to handling objects. Dropping, banging, and throwing are usually the first indications. The classic example of this change occurs when a seven-month-old drops a spoon or other small object from a high chair and then looks to see where it went. This overtly simple action turns out to be surprisingly intense and long-lasting, and the pattern, which began with basic hand moments at around ten weeks of age, will continue to be a primary focus for the healthy child right on through to about age two.

How to Do It

1. Tie toys to your baby's stroller or high chair. Watch his reactions closely during this play. **Safety note: Never leave your baby unattended with the ribbon, yarn, string, or long shoelaces. Remove them promptly when you are finished with this activity.**

2. After your baby throws the toy, you can teach him to retrieve it by himself by pulling on the line.

3. If you laugh and react positively to his new dropping, throwing, and retrieving skills, he is likely to enjoy the process over and over again.

Out of Sight, but Not Out of Mind

Your baby will notice when items go missing, particularly toys!

Materials

Washcloth
Small, safe toy

Behind the Scenes

While you are likely to love this new awareness of objects, you will probably not find it enjoyable if you need to be out of the room, even for a short time. There are different ways to cope with your baby's new awareness, and one effective idea is to play a leave-the-room game and return quickly each time.

Research Roundup!

From respected authority Penelope Leach in her well-known book *Your Baby & Child: From Birth to Age Five*, there is specific information about the six- to seven-month stage. She describes the baby as liking to be with the parent so much that she also dislikes it when the parent leaves. She explains that the baby might "reach a point, at around eight or nine months, when she tries to keep you in sight every moment of her waking day; when she cannot she may be uneasy, tearful or even panic-stricken." She ends her explanation by saying, "Psychologists call this reaction *separation anxiety*." Her main point is, "When the baby loses sight of you, she minds. You are the center of her world, the mirror in which she sees herself and everything else." As far as she is concerned, you might be gone forever. Different from the game with the objects disappearing, you are extremely important, and she has no ability at this time to understand that you will for sure be coming back.

Ten

Our number system is based on the number ten, so this is a wonderful time to introduce this numerical concept to your baby.

Materials

10 items, such as paper cups or blocks

Behind the Scenes

Focusing on number ten is a good reminder about how basic ten is to so much of what we do and experience. Noticing and counting numbers of items together can help stimulate all the other areas of development, such as fine motor, social-emotional, language, and self-esteem. While this activity is not meant for teaching a baby to count, it is designed for exposure to this important basic language. Because hearing words of all kinds is beneficial, any that lay the groundwork for later learning are especially helpful.

Research Roundup!

Although very young children can't count yet, using math language every day supports their developing math vocabulary and understanding. In her article "More, All, Gone Empty, Full: Math Talk Every Day in Every Way," Jan Greenberg suggests using math language in a variety of settings: at home, at the grocery store, while walking in the neighborhood.

Get Ready for Motor Skills with Movement and Eye-Hand Expertise

Sitting and Playing

To perfect sitting, give your baby opportunities to sit. Either prop your baby on a sofa next to you or allow him to sit supported. Never leave your baby unattended.

Materials

Items for your baby to manipulate, such as a set of blocks, plastic spoons, or small plastic cups

Behind the Scenes

You are laying the groundwork for sitting and practicing eye-hand coordination with this activity, which are two important skills for your baby.

Research Roundup!

"Motor skills do not develop miraculously from one day to the next" and are, instead, taught, according to Jane E. Clark

---

How to Do It

1. Start with your baby's ten fingers.

2. Sing, "One little, two little, three little fingers . . . ," as you move each one of your baby's little fingers.

3. You might also count ten paper cups together.

4. In a restaurant, you might want to count ten sugar packets. In a doctor's office, you could count ten magazines. Wherever you are, look for items to count to encourage your baby's understanding of counting and numbers.

How to Do It

1. Give your baby a small object to hold in each hand. He may bang the two together.

2. Offer your baby a third related object.

3. At first he may not know what to do, but in time your baby will learn to set one object down to pick up the new one. He may also give one object to you or figure out how to hold two items in the same hand.

in "On the Problem of Motor Skill Development." Because no one, she says, consciously teaches an infant how to "sit or stand, a belief emerges that maturation is the cause." However, in reality, all of these milestones require environmental support for their appearance, she asserts. This support is not formal and should feel natural to both baby and parent. The environment needs to be 'just good enough' for the behaviors to appear. Sedentary life is a new and big intrusion on life today, and we all have to guard against it to keep it from hurting motor-skills development, a process that needs encouragement in infancy and continues to need direction throughout the elementary school years.

Crawling and Playing

It is a good idea to encourage the crawling position. You can do this by gently supporting your baby around the middle with your arms. You can also place him on a roll-shaped pillow.

Materials
A favorite toy
Circular pillow (optional)

Behind the Scenes
During every stage, you will see your baby become happier, and much of that pleasure comes from his movement. Imagine how exciting life becomes for your baby. He goes from lying down to sitting up and beginning to get around to new and different places.

Research Roundup!
"The skills learned from one ability—like crawling—are not the same skills that will help a baby learn to walk. . . . Toddlers give up a lot of speed, knowledge, and competence to walk. The payoff is the ability to do two things at once—move and carry things—and to see more from the relative increase in height," according to "Rocking and Rolling: Learning to Move" by Sandra Petersen, Emily J. Adams, and Linda Gillespie. Increasing opportunities for movement is the key because that provides a baby on the move more chances to grow, test, and refine motor skills.

How to Do It

1. Place a toy on the floor.

2. Place your baby near the toy in a comfortable crawling position, either supported or not. **Safety note:** If you choose to use a pillow for this activity, do not leave your child unattended with the pillow.

3. Encourage him to get the toy.

4. Move the toy to another spot and encourage your baby to crawl to it.

5. Keep playing as long as you and your baby continue to enjoy it.

Pulling Up

Your baby will pull to standing naturally. Popular places to pull up include in his crib while holding on to a crib bar, at a low table, or by a sturdy shelf.

Materials

Toys or other safe items

Behind the Scenes

Pulling up is a major self-esteem–building milestone, due to baby's happiness with being able to see the world from a different point of view. Your joy can magnify the value of this accomplishment. Other people can positively reinforce this milestone, but nothing will mean as much to your baby as the pride that only a parent or primary caregiver can give.

Research Roundup!

"Giving Your Child Positive Attention," from Boys Town Research Hospital, says that babies need love, attention, consistency, playfulness, and patience as they grow. They start moving everywhere, and because they are naturally curious, they also start to reach out and touch all sorts of things. This sometimes causes trouble and at the very least makes parents nervous. As your baby starts to move about, it is important to use gentle ways to remove him from dangerous situations and to guide him back to a safe place. While adults often wish that their babies would stop doing certain things, the idea is to be one step ahead and always keep looking for safe and productive places for your baby to play.

How to Do It

1. Clear the table or shelf of all breakable items.

2. Replace the items with toys or toylike items that he will enjoy for play.

3. Watch your baby pull up and reach for the items. Always be there for needed help, encouragement, and safety.

Knee-Up

Sit with your baby on your knee, facing you. This is a great place for him to practice sitting balance.

Materials

None

Behind the Scenes

Bouncing your little one on your knee comes naturally. This natural play prepares your baby for the next big milestone: sitting! All of your interactions with your baby are formative in one way or another. Too little interaction slows a baby's progress, and with infant seats and strollers so available today for helpful use, parents and other caregivers must always be on the lookout for movement opportunities of all kinds.

How to Do It

1. Hold your baby's hands and give him all the support he needs. Gradually let go of one hand if he balances and looks comfortable.

2. As you go through this process, gently bounce your knee.

3. As your baby is put off balance, he will hold on to you and right himself.

4. As your baby gains balance, he will be strengthening his back muscles for sitting.

5. Stay in tune with your baby as you play, bounce, and encourage independent sitting. Only continue with this play if your baby enjoys it. He will gain balance when he is ready.

Research Roundup!

"Babies can learn music by feeling it as well as hearing it," according to the American Association for the Advancement of Science website. Psychologist Laurel Trainor of McMaster University in Canada and her colleagues asked mothers to bounce their babies to a rhythm. Half of the babies were bounced on every second beat and half on every third. Later, when the babies heard the same rhythms, they showed clear preference for the patterns to which they were bounced. While hearing provides one dimension for learning, feeling in this study is what made the difference to the success of the learning.

You Do, I Do Too!

When you copy your baby's movements, you encourage him to try new and different ones. In most situations, adults tell babies what to do. In this one, your baby in his own way will be telling you what to do.

Materials

None

Behind the Scenes

At this stage, ability is newly combined with initiative. The more you play this game, the more your options will grow. Pointing, changing objects from one hand to another, and the pincer grasp are just three examples of behaviors that are likely to appear for you to copy and enjoy together.

How to Do It

1. Gently place your baby on the floor.

2. Get in the same or a similar position.

3. However your baby moves and whatever he does, make the same sounds and movements. Your baby will enjoy this activity for the independence it allows him.

In the article "Age-Related Changes in Deferred Imitation between 6 and 9 Months of Age" by researcher Jane S. Herbert and her colleagues, we learn about memory development. The experimenter first performed a single action with one object with both age groups for the purpose of imitation. Infants of both ages imitated that same action immediately and performed equally well. When the same infants were tested again after a twenty-four-hour delay, only the nine-month-olds imitated successfully. While this study at first glance might not seem important, it pointed out important differences in memory development between the six-month and nine-month-old stages.

Grow Social Skills with Fun Interactions

New Foods

All of your baby's nutrition can be provided adequately from nursing or bottle-feeding. There is no nutritional need for specific foods. However, soft fresh fruit pieces and freshly cooked vegetables make excellent food choices for your baby to try. **Make sure the pieces are not too big to cause choking.**

Materials

Small pieces of fruit, such as banana, peach, peeled pear, strawberries, or kiwi

Small pieces of cooked vegetables, such as potatoes, carrots, peas, squash, zucchini, or green beans

Behind the Scenes

Eating together with your baby is beneficial. Enjoying meals together will grow your baby's communication skills and bonding.

How to Do It

1. Place some small food pieces on your baby's highchair.

2. Encourage your baby to pick up one piece at a time and eat the soft, bite-sized pieces.

3. Now it's your turn. Have a section on the table for your food pieces and eat some bites after your baby takes his.

4. Watch your baby's reaction and continue to enjoy sampling different foods together.

Research Roundup!

In "Promoting Healthy Eating Habits Right from the Start" by Rebecca Parlakian and Claire Lerner, the feeding relationship is defined by the relationship that parent and child (or caregiver and child) establish around food. This dynamic concept is about "much more than providing nutrients to a child," they say, and encompasses to a large extent *sharing power*, a concept that shapes a child's lifelong eating habits. "For a child to develop a healthy approach to eating from birth, adult and child must share responsibility during feeding." Research suggests that parents begin to establish regular meal- and snack times for children between nine and twelve months old.

Hats Off

Most babies love to have hats placed on their heads. Your baby will also enjoy seeing you modeling different hats on your head.

Materials
Several hats of your choice

Behind the Scenes
The big surprise for you is likely to be seeing your baby's preference. While you may not expect a like or dislike for one hat over another, you are likely to see that your baby does express a preference.

Research Roundup!
In a study dubbed "the Goldilocks effect," babies were found to "seek out situations with just the right amount of surprise or complexity," according to researchers from the University of Rochester. The evidence from the study supports the idea that babies "learn best from social interaction," says Celeste Kidd, lead author of the study. "They are not passive sponges. They are active information seekers looking for the best information they can find."

How to Do It

1. Sit with your baby in front of a mirror with the hats beside you.

2. One at a time, take each hat and place it on your baby's head.

3. Notice his response.

4. Then take each hat, also one at a time, and place it on your head.

5. Notice your baby's response. Continue the play as long as your baby enjoys it. He may prefer seeing and touching the hats, so allow him to explore as much as he's interested.

See It, Touch It

Your baby is interested in touching everything in sight. This is your opportunity to help him find new and different things to touch and to explain their textures.

How to Do It

1. Hold your baby and take him on a walk around your house.

2. Stop at different items and explain them as rough, smooth, warm, cold, hard, soft, and any other description that comes to mind.

3. Elaborate with your language and point out as many opposites as you can. Here are some suggestions: a mirror is hard, and pillows are soft. A refrigerator is cold, and a cushion is warm. Tables are hard, and sofas are soft. Beards are rough, and hands are smooth.

Materials

None

Research Roundup!

The article "Some Things to Learn from Learning through Touch" by Kate Moss is based on the book *Learning Through Touch* by Mike McLinden and Stephen McCall, who state that our largest organ is our skin, and, among other functions, it is also the location of the tactile receptors in our body. Touch is designed to seek out and acquire information, typically using the hands. "As the child's vision and motor skills develop, Moss says, a typical baby begins to incorporate more and more strategies for exploring objects with the hands. Think about the ways most babies spend their time. They are constantly interacting with objects in their world—reaching and grasping, banging and batting, putting together, and taking apart.

Inclined Plane Rolling

There are several ways to set up an inclined plane. One is to take a cutting board and lean it on two, three, or four books. Another is to lean a large book against a stack of other books.

Materials

Cutting board or coffee-table book
Books
Tennis ball

Behind the Scenes

With this activity you have the option of adjusting the incline, ranging in variations from slight to steep. While your baby is too young to understand the related speed of the ball, he will enjoy experiencing the results of the variations, and that is significant. Baby learning comes from experiences, and the subtlety of this one will make an impact.

How to Do It

1. Set up your inclined plane with your baby watching you.

2. Roll a ball down the inclined plane.

3. Invite your baby to place the ball on the high end of the plane so that it will roll down.

4. Guide your baby to find the ball and bring it back to you to play again.

5. Repeat the activity for as long as you and your baby continue to enjoy it.

Research Roundup!

Infants learn much language well before they speak, says Marianella Casasola, associate professor in the Department of Human Development at Cornell University. Dr. Casasola works in a completely social environment, and, except for the computers and other technical equipment, her research space or "baby lab" resembles an open, baby-friendly play area. As described by Kimberly Kopko in her article on Dr. Casasola's work, without a lot of structure and well-versed in phonology (the sound system of language), Casasola picks up many details that others may miss.

The Sunglasses Routine

This game fits into the peekaboo variety of play and will provide a fun activity for you and your baby.

Materials
Sunglasses

Behind the Scenes
Baby games that promote turn taking are especially valuable. The activity is very basic, but interacting in conversational ways is effective for your baby's development.

Research Roundup!
Dr. Caspar Addyman of Goldsmiths, University of London, is known at the university as the baby laughter researcher. He has been acknowledged for his landmark work linking the ability of children to see the funny side of an event with profound developments inside the brain. From his Baby Laughter Project, which has surveyed parents from more than twenty countries, he has concluded that peekaboo is a perfect game for showing how children at varying stages of development understand the same phenomenon differently. He explains that very young children around six months of age can look shocked and startled at peekaboo, because they can think that not being able to see the person's face or an object means that the person or object has actually disappeared. However, once a child understands at about six to eight months that one thing can hide something else, then peekaboo becomes a much more fun experience and all about the anticipation of when the person or object is going to come back into view.

How to Do It

1. Sit with your baby on a sofa or comfortable chair.

2. Put on your sunglasses.

3. Have your baby remove your sunglasses or remove them yourself.

4. As you (or your baby) remove them, say, "Peekaboo, I see you."

5. Put the glasses back on and play again.

6. Continue the play for as long as you and your baby enjoy it.

Welcome Language Growth with Songs, Words, and Books

Dance Little Baby

Your baby will learn new vocabulary by experiencing the words through dance. Singing the song and moving your baby in different directions will help your baby build his language learning.

Materials
None

Behind the Scenes
Babbles, vocalizations that sound like words, and *ma-ma* and *da-da* are likely to be prevalent now. Echo your baby's babbles and add words as well. Rich language is the right form of communication most beneficial for your baby.

1. Sing the words to the following song, and move your baby in the directions as marked.

   Dance Little Baby

   Dance little baby (Dance with your baby)

   Dance up high (Hold your baby over your head)

   Never mind baby (Dance with your baby)

   Mother (or father) *is by* (Hug your baby)

   Up to the ceiling (Hold your baby over your head)

   Down to the ground (Dance your baby down to the floor)

   Backward (Move your baby backward)

   And forward (Move your baby forward)

   Round and round (Move your baby round and round)

2. Continue as long as your baby is enjoying the activity.

Research Roundup!

Researchers who previously believed that infants between six and nine months of age were able to understand only sounds and not words have found evidence to discredit this idea, according to researchers Elika Bergelson and Daniel Swingley. While babies typically do not speak or even gesture meaningfully before ten or eleven months, they understand more than most people realize. From both simple picture and more complex-image tests, the researchers found understanding for both the six- and nine-month-old babies. In addition, the level of comprehension shown seemed to remain constant until it jumped quite a lot by about fourteen months old.

Reading Time III

Board books with simple pictures and large print are durable and great for this activity. You can make your own board books out of old birthday and holiday cards. Laminate them for extra protection if you want, then hole-punch them along the left sides and run yarn through the holes to hold them together.

Materials

Board books

Birthday and holiday cards (optional)

Clear contact paper (optional)

Hole punch (adult use only, optional)

Yarn (optional)

Behind the Scenes

Reading to your baby provides the opportunity for advanced language that you might not necessarily use in everyday communication. It also generates closeness for the two of you and presents a chance to watch for clues of understanding and paying attention. Your little one may want to turn the pages, and you might hear some language responses to certain pages or pictures.

Research Roundup!

Similar advice comes from my book *Constructive Parenting*. Reading to babies in this six- to twelve-month-old age range teaches the value of books and the learning that they inspire. Another benefit is teaching young children the value of print, or *print awareness*. Picture books with clear, detailed pictures of recognizable people and objects for your child to learn to name are recommended. In addition, your baby will benefit from seeing you hold a book the proper way, turn pages from left to right, and point out interesting pictures and words.

How to Do It

1. Sit comfortably with your baby.

2. Read a board book, bought or homemade, to your baby.

3. Point out bright pictures and interesting words.

4. Explain whatever you can to enhance your baby's learning. Remember, this is a communication activity in which you continue to check that your baby is understanding on his level.

Head, Shoulders, Knees, and Toes II

Naming parts of the body is an excellent way to expand your baby's vocabulary. Touching each part when you name it also enhances the learning experience.

Materials

None

Behind the Scenes

Repetition enhances learning for your baby, and songs with built-in repetitions make excellent learning tools.

Research Roundup!

In my book *Baby and Toddler Learning Fun,* the focus is on learning the basic concepts of colors, letters, numbers, shapes, and reading during the years from birth to eighteen months, and repetition is referenced many times as a valuable learning strategy. Numerals are learned first as symbols before the corresponding numerical concepts are internalized. Both are best "introduced and reinforced by activities emphasizing repetition and

How to Do It

1. Sit your baby comfortably next to you and sing this popular song.

2. Use your baby's hands to point to each part on his body as named in the song.

   Head, shoulders, knees, and toes, knees and toes.
   Head, shoulders, knees, and toes, knees and toes.
   Eyes and ears and mouth and nose.
   Head, shoulders, knees, and toes, knees and toes.

familiarity." According to Dr. Bruce Perry, who was quoted on PBS's KBYU Eleven, "repetition is key to the development of a child's brain. Repetition leads to skill mastery, which increases confidence and builds self-esteem."

Fingerplay of Your Choice

Fingerplays are excellent tools for teaching your baby new vocabulary. The actual finger and hand motions reinforce the meaning of the words.

How to Do It

1. Sing the song, "The Eensy Weensy Spider." Some know it better with the words *itsy bitsy.*

2. Be sure to do the corresponding finger and hand movements as marked.

   The eensy weensy spider went up the water spout.
   (Touch opposite thumbs to forefingers and forefingers to thumbs)
   Down came the rain and washed the spider out.
   (Move hands down by wiggling fingers)
   Out came the sun and dried up all the rain.
   (Move hands out to each side and move back and forth from left to right)
   And the eensy weensy spider went up the spout again.
   (Touch opposite thumbs to forefingers and forefingers to thumbs)

Materials
None

Behind the Scenes
With baby beginning to understand the concepts of *up* and *down*, this is a perfect learning song and is enhanced by repetition. The rhyming format is catchy, and the finger and hand movements are fun.

Research Roundup!
While this rhyme has a wonderful message about starting all over again when things go wrong, it also has another purpose for this six- to twelve-month baby level—introducing language sounds. According to information collected by the Northport-East Northport Public Library for their "Road to Reading" program, this rhyme, which is also a fingerplay and song, and all of the others they have selected, provide a "wonderful rhythm and word play to help familiarize your child with the wide variety of sounds in spoken language." The concept, they say, is *phonemic awareness*—the ability to segment and manipulate the sounds, and a key component of reading readiness.

See It, Hear It, Explain It

Your baby is absorbing a great many vocabulary words. The best way to foster this kind of learning is to keep talking to your baby.

Materials

None

Behind the Scenes

Because your baby cannot understand all the big words you use, there is a tendency to try not to use them. However, it is best to go against that feeling and keep talking, describing, and explaining to your baby what you are doing.

Research Roundup!

Children learn language from hearing it, and they start this process at birth or even before. The landmark study that builds on this concept is "Talking to Children Matters: Early Language Experience Strengthens Processing and Builds Vocabulary" by researchers Adriana Weisleder and Anne Fernald. It focuses on the quantity and quality of parent language with babies. Through a natural system of recording parent-infant speech, they were able to tell that those parents who talked more to their babies at nineteen months old had children by twenty-four months who were "more efficient in processing familiar words and had larger expressive vocabularies." While this particular study starts measurement at nineteen months of age and shows dramatic effects by outcomes at twenty-four months, it follows many other previous studies that have established the beginnings of baby hearing at about seven months of gestation and also have documented much other baby-language development that occurs all through the first year.

How to Do It

1. Whatever you are doing, explain it in as much detail as possible to your baby.

2. If you are cooking, talk about each step. If you are dressing your baby, talk about the clothes and how you are putting them on him.

3. The more words and details you add to your explanations, the more beneficial the vocabulary building will be to your baby.

Embellish Self-Esteem Development with All Your Joy

Where Is Baby?

The more attention and appreciation you shower on your baby, the better he will feel about himself. Using the word *baby* is okay in the beginning, but then it is best to switch to your baby's name.

Materials
Dishtowel

Behind the Scenes
Peekaboo shows up in many forms throughout childhood. For this age and stage, this quick and easy appear-disappear interaction provides just the right amount of excitement to focus attention on your baby.

Research Roundup!
"12 Fun Baby Learning Games," written by Nicci Micco for parenting.com, shows how important positive parent-child interaction is. While health is, of course, the main goal, being smart is important too; and it is parents who make the biggest difference in how information is conveyed. Science clearly shows that baby's brain development depends largely on his early experiences. "You are the best toy in the room," Micco quotes Gina Lebedeva, PhD, director of translation, outreach, and education at the University of Washington's Institute for Learning and Brain Sciences as saying, "Our brains have evolved to learn from other brains." Just engaging a baby in positive, everyday ways is exactly what helps build the trillions of brain connections that lead to language development, problem-solving skills, and the emotional development that goes along with it. The key is to have fun with your little one as you spend meaningful time together.

How to Do It

1. Place a hand towel or a dishtowel in front of your baby's face.

2. Ask, "Where is baby?"

3. Take the towel away and say, "Here you are."

4. You can also do the activity with "Where is Mommy?" or "Where is Daddy?" or "Where is Grandma?"

5. Repeat these actions as often as you wish.

Record-a-Sound

Your baby's voice is interesting to both of you, so recording your baby making sounds and then watching the video together will be great fun. Your baby may find this to be a favorite activity.

Materials
Smartphone or other recording device

Behind the Scenes
Self-esteem grows from positive reinforcement. The tricky part is being genuine, and your baby knows the difference. What to do? From the beginning, avoid using generalizations such as "good

boy" and "good job." Start with specifics, such as, "What a cute little sound!" and "You said *ba-ba-ba.*"

Research Roundup!

Research led by University of British Columbia postdoctoral fellow Judit Gervain found that, while baby's first words are often *mama* and *dada*, much to the delight of parents, scientists now think they know why. Going beyond the obvious, that parents are around a lot and that babies are drawn to them, it turns out that repeated syllables are what make the difference. From similar patterns noted in many other languages, the data was clear. The study focused on comparing the difference between words with repeating syllables like *mubaba* and *penana* with ones without them like *mubage* and *penaku*, and showed that brain activity increased in specific areas whenever the syllable-repetitious words were played.

Magazine Time

Your baby enjoys looking at pictures. You may already have some children's magazines available, but if not, you can use any magazine of your choice for this activity.

Materials

Magazines

Behind the Scenes

Any joy you express while spending time with your baby is exactly what will naturally add to his self-esteem. The communication between the two of you is vital to his growth.

Research Roundup!

Playthings do not have to be expensive or new, says Jenn Berman, PhD, in the article "10 Reasons Play Makes Babies Smarter." Ideally toys should not be electronic because that means the toy is likely doing most of the work. Berman explains, "Some active toys—the ones with the bells and whistles—prompt kids to sit back and be entertained by pushing buttons. But passive toys make for active kids." When the toy is simple, a child is forced to be "creative, dynamic and engaged," and that is exactly what enables and promotes development.

How to Do It

1. Start to record when you hear your baby making sounds.

2. Play back the video that you have recorded.

3. This is likely to stimulate your baby to say more sounds.

4. Continue making recordings of your baby and playing them back for him as long as he enjoys it.

How to Do It

1. Look through any magazine you have handy.

2. Point out interesting pictures and explain them in a natural way.

3. Let your baby turn pages if he's interested. He may point at pictures, so talk to him in detail about anything that interests him.

Baby's First Poem

This poem has been especially designed for your baby to learn simple concepts by experiencing them. Being able to show this learning is what packs this activity with self-esteem–building power.

Materials

None

How to Do It

1. Starting with the first part of the poem, say the words to your baby and lead him through the actions with his fingers, hands, and whole-body movements.

2. As you see and experience the words together, show your happiness and joy.

3. Repeat the first stanza often before you go on to the second part. Recognition of the words and familiarity with the actions for both of you is what will increase the value of the poem each time you play.

One plus one equals two (Bring two forefingers to the front)
Two plus two equals four (Bring first and second forefingers to the front)
Right now I don't know anymore
I can stand up (Stand up your baby)
I can sit down (Sit down your baby)
I can move my whole self all around (Turn your baby all around)

I can raise my right hand (Raise your baby's right hand)
I can raise my left hand too (Raise your baby's left hand)
That's not all that I can do
I can raise my right foot (Raise your baby's right foot)
I can raise my left foot (Raise your baby's left foot)
I can touch my toes (Touch your baby's toes)
And I can touch my nose (Touch your baby's nose)

I can clap my hands (Clap your baby's hands)
Pat my head (Pat your baby's head)
Cover my eyes (Cover your baby's eyes)
And make peekaboo (Uncover your baby's eyes)
That's a lot of things I can do
I wave hi (Wave your baby's hand)
But now I say, "Bye-bye" (Wave your baby's hand)

Source: From *Teaching with Toys* by Sally Goldberg

Behind the Scenes

Because this poem is long, with each part focusing on different types of actions, this activity should be broken down into small segments by stanzas. Taken together, the poem reflects accomplishments and the resultant self-esteem that grows from this kind of personal baby experience.

Research Roundup!

I wrote the poem, which was published in my book *Teaching with Toys*, while immersed in the joy of seeing all the new actions my baby was doing, and so the rhymes had their own way of coming together. The whole concept fell into the language-stimulation category; the words were fun to say, and they also had natural actions that went with them. The objective is to provide interaction for parent and baby, centered around the things baby can do or is learning to do.

The Grand Old Duke of York

This is a well-known rhyme that teaches your baby concepts as he experiences them. The correct position for enjoying this activity is bouncing your baby on your knee.

Materials

None

Behind the Scenes

You can talk to your baby about being *up* and *down*, but experiencing the concepts by movement is best. The more you two engage in this activity, the stronger the benefits of familiarity. Your baby's "bouncing" good time will be a sign of inner pride.

Research Roundup!

This poem's rhythm and fun wordplay can help familiarize a child with a wide variety of sounds in spoken language. The emphasis on the words *up* and *down* and being able to learn and understand their meanings from the exaggerated movements can grow your child's understanding of these concepts.

How to Do It

1. Sing this well-known rhyme/song to your baby.

2. Move his body according to the motions as marked.

The Grand Old Duke of York

The grand old duke of York
    (Gently bounce your baby)
He had ten thousand men
    (Bounce your baby)
He marched them up the hill
    (Move your baby up)
*And he marched them down
    again* (Carefully move your
    baby down)
When you're up, you're up
    (Move your baby up)
*And when you're down, you're
    down* (Move your baby down)
*And when you're only halfway
    up* (Move your baby halfway
    up)
You're neither up nor down
    (Move your baby up, then
    down)

Fun Baby Learning Games

4 Nine to Twelve Months

Movement and understanding are increasing rapidly with your baby. Remembering objects out of sight is also a major developmental leap. Utterances and even words represent communication, and your baby is understanding new words she hears spoken.

Crawling is frequent as your baby gains new independence of movement, and first steps might even be part of the picture. This is an especially good time for you to introduce your baby to all kinds of sounds, words, songs, and maybe some dances.

Increased mobility helps with your baby's desire for exploration. Remembering friends and family, she will want to get to know more people. Newness is key. Whatever your baby is getting into, try to explain in as much detail as possible what she is experiencing and seeing. Enrich her play by introducing more bright colors, music, textures, delicious natural foods, and tempting aromas.

On the Move and Happy Too!

Crawling to get around is wonderful for your baby's growth in many areas. It opens up a whole new world of possibilities, and your baby knows that. Find your activity day by day, week by week, or any time you choose. Little by little, watch all the growth with pulling up, cruising, and eventually walking. Wow, look at your happy baby go!

Milestones of Development

- Uncovers a hidden object
- Explores an object in a number of ways
- Understands that objects have a front, back, top, and bottom
- Rolls or pushes an object
- Walks while holding on to furniture
- Walks
- Responds playfully to a mirror

- Drinks from a cup
- Responds to praise and positive attention
- Enjoys simple play
- Begins to understand and respond to one- or two-word phrases other than her name
- Responds to *no* and *sit down*
- Says sounds and occasional words
- Enjoys simple songs

Watch for Cognitive Growth as Your Baby Explores

Boxes

Boxes have a great allure for babies. Have fun with whatever ones you have available. You can change your play from week to week as new containers arrive at your house.

Materials
Boxes, such as small cartons or shoe boxes

Behind the Scenes
Everyone says that babies at one year of age have more fun with the boxes of presents than with the presents themselves. This game is a natural way to play . . . and much cheaper too!

Research Roundup!
"Why Do Babies Like Boxes Best?" by Linda Gillespie in *Young Children* explains why the famous "box" that houses a gift is usually the biggest hit of all for a one-year-old, and the answer is directly related to this stage of development. Most prominent is the desire to explore toys and objects in meaningful ways. Now the baby can turn something over, put it inside something else, give it to others, and handle it in many ways. What about the toy inside? Oh, that is one-dimensional. While it might look cute and original to an adult, it does not offer the endless opportunities of the box or several boxes for exploring with all the senses.

How to Do It

1. Place smaller boxes inside larger ones.

2. Include in the smallest box a surprise such as a doll, toy car, or other interesting object.

3. Have fun with your baby as you both take turns opening boxes from the largest to the smallest.

Flashlight Fun

Small stuffed animals will surprise your baby in this activity. Dolls of similar sizes will also be fine. Another good choice is a group of small toy cars.

Materials

Small stuffed animals, dolls, or toy cars
Flashlight

Behind the Scenes

Because your baby is quite responsive now, it is beneficial to be creative by using new and different ways to experience simple objects. Surprise your baby by helping her see familiar toys in a new way.

Research Roundup!

A research study from Johns Hopkins University explains that babies have a built-in expectation for how things operate, and when those expectations are defied, they learn better. Lead researcher Aimee Stahl, a PhD candidate at Johns Hopkins, finds, "Thirty years of research on infant cognition has shown that babies look longer when a situation appears to be surprising rather than a predictable event." The researchers found that babies are born with innate knowledge that helps them to learn new things, but the way they learn best is when an object or event does something unexpected or surprising. "Infants focus more intensely and for longer periods on objects that don't behave in a predictable manner," Stahl added.

How to Do It

1. Set up a line of your selected toys against a wall.

2. Shine a flashlight on one of the toys.

3. **Hold on to the flashlight for safety reasons.** Be careful not to shine it in anyone's eyes. Most cannot hurt your eyes, but some today are made with very strong lights that can cause harm.

4. Shine the light on different toys for your baby, and switch the types of toys you are using to continue her play.

Blow the Cotton

This game will work best as you and your baby sit across the table from each other. You will need two straws, one for each of you, and more cotton balls.

Materials

2 straws
Cotton balls

Behind the Scenes

This activity provides your baby an example of cause and effect. It also lays the groundwork for learning problem-solving strategies. A bonus benefit is the muscle strength your baby will build in the mouth area.

How to Do It

1. Take turns blowing through your straws to send the cotton balls across the table.

2. Play back and forth with the cotton balls for as long as you two continue to have fun.

Research Roundup!

Mouths have touch receptors (cells that give your brain information about the world around you through touch), which are highly concentrated in the lips, according to "Mouth Activities," an article on the Occupational Therapy for Children website. These receptors "correlate to a larger area of the brain that receives messages from the lips . . . compared to other less sensitive areas of the body. More brain power is spent interpreting touch sensations from the lips . . . than from other areas of the body that have touch cell receptors." This seemingly simple activity also helps grow the muscles used for blowing that help make up those needed for having strong neck, chest, stomach, and back control.

Stick to It

While it is easy to be interactive with your baby, it is more difficult to find an activity that is exploratory, self-contained, and fun for her to do on her own. You will find that the sticky side of contact paper provides such an opportunity.

Materials

9" x 12" sheet of contact paper
Adhesive tape
Uncooked pasta, such as penne rigatoni, spirals, shells, and bowties

Behind the Scenes

What's so special about this activity is that you can watch your baby grow with it. While at first all pasta placements will be random, in time there will be more order and choice about where your baby places each piece. Because her pincer grasp is developing, pieces of dry pasta will be interesting to touch and easy to manipulate.

Research Roundup!

Priscila Cacola, assistant professor of kinesiology at the University of Texas at Arlington, says that developing a child's motor skills is extremely important because motor development is actually the mediator of cognitive, social, and emotional development. "Good motor skills predict a whole lot later in life, so it might be something that all of us should be concerned about early in a child's life," she says.

How to Do It

1. Cut a sheet of contact paper.
2. Place it sticky side up on your baby's high chair or on a table at which she can sit comfortably.
3. Tape it so that it does not move around.
4. Give your baby a small bowlful of pasta. **Safety note: Stay close to make sure your baby doesn't choke on the pasta pieces.**
5. Tell your baby to stick the pasta on the sticky side of the contact paper.
6. She will be able to move the pieces around and create interesting designs.

Tent

If exploring objects out in the open keeps your baby busy for hours on end, she will thoroughly enjoy play when you start hiding objects. Surprise is one of the major characteristics of effective play.

Materials
Chair or small table
Blanket or tablecloth
5 interesting objects

Behind the Scenes
This is another version of the ever-fun and effective peekaboo activity as your baby wonders what will happen next. Your baby takes the lead by deciding how to enjoy the items under the blanket or tablecloth, and you follow with your joy about her decisions.

Research Roundup!
Babies laugh a lot, and their reasons change as they grow and develop, says Caspar Addyman, PhD. According to his work, simple visual and tactile stimuli work best on younger babies (four to five months old), while it takes more involved social games, such as peekaboo, to cause older babies to laugh. That is because the laughing response changes as a baby grows. Babies under six months laugh because they think something that happened was funny, but from six months on they keep refining their understanding of the disappearing and reappearing item and laugh more in tune with the surprise and complexity of the play.

Gross-Motor and Fine-Motor Progress with Baby on the Move

Raisins and Cereal

These bite-sized snacks are delicious, healthy, and fun for your baby to eat. The more you use this activity with your baby, the more she will develop a pincer grasp.

Materials
Raisins, cereal, or other natural fruit pieces

Behind the Scenes

After so much time watching your baby use a full fist to either pick up items or try to pick them up, the pincer grasp is a welcome development. With exposure to appropriate, small, safe food pieces, you will continue to see improvement with this skill. No need to hold back your delight. When you acknowledge this fine-motor achievement, your baby is absorbing and benefiting from your positive reinforcement: "All I need to do is eat a little piece of food, and they think I'm terrific!" This simple response is your baby's fuel to feel great about herself and will help her continue to use and perfect this important new ability.

Research Roundup!

"Importance of the Proper Pincer Grip" on SchoolSparks.com has valuable information about the progression of this fine-motor skill. The *pincer grip*, a common term among educators, therapists, and doctors, is the grasp used with the index finger and thumb to pick up small items. There are typically three different grip stages babies go through as they develop fine-motor skills:

- **Fist grip.** Early on as babies start to reach for and hold items, they do so with their entire fist. A baby will hold an item with a closed fist and keep her thumb on top.

- **Four-finger grip.** As babies continue to gain fine-motor control, they typically progress from using a fist grip to a four-fingered one. Now the baby uses all four fingers together to hold an object against her thumb. This grip gives a child greater control but is still a little clumsy and inefficient.

- **Pincer grip.** Once a baby nears one year old, she develops a strong fine-motor skill that is a true pincer grasp. With this grip, a baby uses only her thumb and index finger to hold and manipulate small objects. With such a grip, a baby or toddler can easily twist, turn pages, open and close, and use crayons or pencils.

Over the Pillows and Through the Hall

Whether your baby is crawling or walking, you can be sure she will be on the move as much as possible. Therefore, play based on movement is likely to be very successful. While a hallway is suggested for this activity, a small and protected room will work.

Materials

Pillows

How to Do It

1. Set your baby in her highchair.

2. Place food on the tray that your baby can pick up easily.

3. Watch your baby enjoy eating the food pieces using her forefinger and thumb.

4. Talk to her about what she's eating and describe in detail the texture, taste, and appearance of her treats.

Behind the Scenes

Pillows can be helpful to assist in your baby's gross motor development, though she does not need to sleep with one in her crib. Using pillows for activities will provide your baby hours of fun and open-ended play.

Research Roundup!

Priscila Cacola worked with other researchers to develop a scale to measure how well different items in a typical home can promote infant motor development. Because all children need an environment that is designed to promote both gross- and fine-motor development, and because parents don't usually think of toys or household items as objects that can foster it, such a scale is very beneficial.

Pull It

Some toys come on a string. Teddy bears and a few other stuffed animals have ribbons or yarn loops as part of their design that you can add to with longer pieces of ribbon or yarn. Whatever kind of pull toy you have or make, your baby will enjoy the movement of the activity. Because your baby is a beginner at walking, make sure she will be able to hold on to the toy easily.

Materials

Teddy bear or other stuffed animal
Ribbon or yarn

Behind the Scenes

Your baby is on the move, exploring! When you add color, texture, and most of all, *purpose*, your baby will love it. There will be pride, too. "Look what I am doing!" will be the inner feeling that she will show by smiling.

Research Roundup!

Penelope Leach, author of *Your Baby & Child: From Birth to Age Five,* says that many babies take their first steps around their first birthday and that it is also perfectly normal for some to start walking a little earlier or later. Children will initially walk with feet wide apart for balance. During those early days, some babies will accidentally

---

How to Do It

1. Place several pillows in a line down your hallway.

2. Put your baby at one end and encourage her to come to you on the other side.

3. Your baby can go over or around the pillows and figure out her own way to get to you.

4. Continue the activity as long as she is enjoying the exercise.

How to Do It

1. Tie ribbon or yarn to a stuffed animal, then give your baby the handle of the pull toy, or tie it to her wrist. **Safety note: Do not leave your baby alone with ribbon or yarn.**

2. Stand on one side of the room and encourage her to pull the toy over to you.

3. When you get it, give the toy back, and then move to the other side of the room. Ask for the toy again.

4. Repeat the activity as long as you both enjoy the play.

get going too fast and fall easily. As they become more confident, they will learn to stop and change directions. Before long they will be able to squat to pick something up and then stand again. Toward the end of the process, they will love playing with push-pull toys, the noisier the better.

Sliding

Your baby is still too small to play on slides at the playground, but you can provide a fun slide of your own using your own two legs.

Materials

None

Behind the Scenes

There's no need to buy a baby slide that will last a short time when you have a built-in one. Many parents also create with their hands and arms a kind of swing that their babies can enjoy at the right size and the right speed. It is terrific to ponder what one active parent and one responsive baby can create together!

Research Roundup!

According to *The New First Three Years of Life* by Burton White, there are no recommended slides for babies under a year-and-a-half old. The first stage of climbing emerges somewhere between eight and ten months, beginning with climbing to "modest heights of eight or nine inches. This height," he explains, "is coincidentally just right for typical stair climbing." Next comes your baby's being able to go up on a low footstool. White says the baby will likely find this capacity to get off the floor very exciting and begin to practice it again and again. Sometime around eleven or twelve months of age comes the ability to climb as much as 16 inches at a time, and this leads to the sofa, but it doesn't stop there. White says there are also the sofa arms to master and the back. The kitchen chair is another challenge, and then that expands to getting on the table and then the counter. It is a joy to watch all this progress, but none of it is especially safe; all of it requires keeping your eyes on your baby at all times.

Come and Get It

Whether crawling or walking, moving to get a toy provides natural fun for your baby. *Toy* is used here loosely because it also includes small pillows or other soft, safe, manageable home objects. They are your tools, and your baby will love exploring and experiencing new things.

Materials

Toys

Behind the Scenes

Action with a purpose is both motivating and fun. This motor activity focuses on all five areas of development. It is specifically designed to increase gross-motor movement, but your baby also has the opportunity for cognitive growth from figuring out how to get to a wanted object. Your interactions together are social, and much language is included. Last but not least, with every successful reach-and-grasp endeavor comes your baby's wonderful feeling of accomplishment. Good for your baby's growth and development and great fun for you both, there is also the added advantage of having nothing to buy and always more ways to create the fun.

Research Roundup!

According to *Teaching with the Brain in Mind* by Eric Jensen, the educational and scientific communities have largely long believed that thinking and movement should be separate. However, today the tides have turned, and there is evidence that there is a strong connection between movement and improved cognition. This kind of pairing is considered to be an effective strategy for learning, memory, and motivation; and current leaders in the field are beginning to advocate for more movement in the learning process.

How to Do It

1. Lead your baby to one end of the room. You go to the other end.

2. Call her to come to you to get the toy you are holding.

3. Bring her back across the room and then return to your spot.

4. Show your baby another toy or other home item, and call her to you just the same.

Enjoy Social Interactions at Every Turn

The Conversation

Whenever your baby is with you, it is important to pay attention to her. Include her in your day-to-day activities as much as possible.

Materials

None

Behind the Scenes

With car seat/stroller life so common these days, it is easy to keep your baby out of the big social picture. While it will not always be possible to include your little one in conversation, be aware of her possible isolation and make intentional overtures to your baby whenever you can.

Research Roundup!

Catherine E. Snow did important research about mother-baby conversations, as reported in "The Development of Conversation Between Mothers and Babies." Her study showed that mothers have a natural way of conversing with babies that starts when babies are about seven months old and continues at the same steady rate up to eighteen months.

How to Do It

1. While you are talking to a friend or neighbor, place your baby where she can see what is going on as you converse.

2. From time to time, direct your conversation to your baby and say something like, "Remember? That was fun." "What do you think of that?"

3. Talk to your little one and include her in conversations to show her that she is part of your social world.

The Introduction

Model social skills with your baby early. While it may not be evident to you now, your baby is taking in everything you say and do. You are providing patterning for your baby that she will observe and utilize soon.

Materials

None

Behind the Scenes

People are a product of individual experiences, and you are the one who can make your baby's early experiences as positive as possible. While bad experiences will happen from time to time, good experiences often require thought and planning.

Research Roundup!

Meeting a baby's needs at this age is very important, and spoiling is not an issue, according to author Penelope Leach in her book *Your Baby & Child: From Birth to Age Five*. The idea of spoiling does not apply to babies; only meeting their needs does. It is not that these little ones are too good to

How to Do It

1. Whenever you meet someone, include your baby in the introduction. Here is the standard greeting:

   "(Older person's name), this is (Baby's name).
   (Baby's name), this is (Older person's name)."

2. Guide your baby to shake hands with the older person if they are both amenable.

3. Avoid illness by keeping your baby's hands clean after she greets people or pets. You may want to keep baby wipes with you at all times for these instances.

get spoiled. It is that they are not grown up or aware enough to be asking for anything with any kind of intent. To act in a manipulative way, a child has to see herself as a separate individual, completely apart from everyone else, and babies do not have this understanding.

Peekaboo II

Here is a game that seems to delight babies of all ages. Parents like it too.

Materials
Hand towel or washcloth

Behind the Scenes
The peekaboo versions you play are becoming more abstract. Although the hands only partially cover and uncover faces, your baby's joy comes from the covering and uncovering motions. This game serves as a good reminder that how you interact with your child makes the difference. Your joy is your child's joy, and the idea is to use it in all its glory whenever and wherever you can!

How to Do It

1. Cover your face with a hand towel or washcloth.

2. Uncover your face and say, "Peekaboo!"

3. You can also cover and uncover your face with your hands or take your baby's hands and cover and uncover her face with them. You could also try covering and uncovering your baby's face with your hands.

Research Roundup!
With regard to babies, the social aspect of play is very important to learning, says Scott Barry Kaufman, PhD, in "10 Insights to Enhance the Joy of Learning" in *Psychology Today*. It is the joy in play that contributes much to a learning experience. Here are some of the best ways to play with your baby.

1. Set it up so that your baby can be successful and not frustrated.

2. Remember that no structure is needed to provide play at its best.

3. Be sure to include freedom for exploring for maximum effectiveness.

I Found You

Finding your baby through this game-like experience will help her to feel loved and secure. Because her first response is to look for you, you can imagine how good it will feel when she finds you.

Materials
None

Behind the Scenes

Babies will often cry if left alone. However, putting an end to that discomfort will provide sheer joy. Doing it over and over for short clips of time and in this playful way should soften the difficulty of such situations when they do happen in life and apart from this game format.

Research Roundup!

Object permanence typically develops between four to seven months of age and involves a baby's understanding that when things disappear, they aren't gone forever, according to Dana Childress, PhD, in "Peek-A-Boo!—Strategies to Teach Object Permanence." This means that if something is completely hidden, your baby will still look for it. This is a very exciting stage because at the same time your baby is also beginning to learn that people continue to exist outside of her sight. With this milestone, however, also comes what is often described as separation anxiety. Babies now fuss and cry when a parent or caregiver leaves the room.

How to Do It

1. Set up an open, safe area for your baby to move around and explore.

2. Once you feel she is happily engaged in the process, leave the room so that you are just out of sight.

3. Return quickly and excitedly say, "I found you."

4. Repeat the process for as long as you and your baby continue to enjoy it. If she isn't enjoying the play, stop the activity and try again at a later date.

Snack Time

While you may think about feeding time as being solely about nutrition, it really is much more. It presents an opportunity to share social time together. Keeping that in mind can give mealtime another focus.

Materials

Small table and chairs or picnic blanket
Plastic cups and paper plates
Snacks

Behind the Scenes

Modern life has created all kinds of baby equipment and special products that keep baby separated from adult life. The more you can include your baby in your daily activities using items as close to adult styles as possible, the better it will be for your baby's growth and development. Social development is a long process, and the more activities you can enjoy together, the smoother that process will be.

How to Do It

1. Set up a finger-food snack time for you and your baby. You can use a child-size table and chairs or set it up like a picnic on the floor or grass.

2. Do your best to make it an attractive eating area for you both.

3. Some recommended snack items that are easy to prepare, are high in nutrition, and are likely to be successful for both of you include:

   - water with lemon or lime squeezed in it. No need to sweeten this drink with sugar. Use cups without lids and help your baby as much as is necessary with the drinking process.

   - soft fruit cut up in bite-sized pieces. Suggested are bananas, peaches, pears, plums, star fruit, mango, papaya, melon, strawberries, blueberries, and raspberries. Fruits such as peaches, pears, and plums should be peeled.

   - soft cooked vegetables cut up in bite-sized pieces. Suggested are potatoes (white and sweet), carrots, squash, zucchini, broccoli, cauliflower, and mushrooms.

   - soft bread cut up in bite-sized pieces. Soft crackers work well too.

   - cereal pieces such as Cheerios. Other cereals that come in bite-sized pieces and that do not have artificial colors, flavors, or preservatives are fine.

   - dried fruit pieces that are made without artificial colors or preservatives, such as raisins, cut up dates, pineapple, and papaya.

Research Roundup!

From the beginning of time, people have eaten together, and mealtimes have often been events when the whole family or settlement or village would come together, according to Robin Fox in "Food and Eating: An Anthropological Perspective." Food is "an occasion for sharing, for distributing and giving, for the expression of altruism, whether from parents to children, children to in-laws, or anyone to visitors and strangers." Food is the most important thing a mother gives her child; from the beginning, breast milk is a substance from her own body, and in most parts of the world, Fox says, mother's milk is still the only safe food for infants. While most parents think that what they are feeding their babies is the most import part of their nutrition training, new research points out that what babies see their parents eating is also an influential factor. In a study by Zoe Liberman and her colleagues, babies learn about eating from social and cultural cues. "Infants view food preferences as meaningfully shared across individuals," and they pay attention to what foods are being eaten around them.

Enrich Baby Language with Lots of Words

Sounds Walk

This is a transition time for your baby from making sounds to saying words, so it is especially beneficial to use as many descriptive words with your baby as possible. One fun way to do this is to describe to your baby all kinds of sounds, such as bird calls or a car's horn. Your descriptions will provide a rich vocabulary for your child.

Materials
Household items that make sound, such as an alarm clock; timer; music box; radio; television; hair dryer; washing machine; and boxes to shake with dry food in them, such as rice, beans, or cereal

Behind the Scenes
When you talk, your baby listens. She will also listen to you when you are talking to others. All the language she hears will provide necessary background for her to one day start speaking words back to you.

How to Do It

1. Take your baby around the house or outside and look for things that make a sound. Every time you find one, describe the sound in detail.

2. Outside you might point out birds, airplanes, dogs barking, children playing, and cars going by. Include as much language as you can, and listen for your baby to make noises, too.

Research Roundup!
"Research Sheds Light on How Babies Learn and Develop Language: Insights for Parents, Teachers, and Educators from Research" by Kimberly Kopko, PhD, talks about the research of Dr. Marianella Casasola, who provided the information from her work at the Cornell University Infant Studies Laboratory, also known as a "baby lab." Her findings add to the knowledge that infants learn to understand words well before they speak. By unlocking some of the complexity behind that learning and showing how the use of novel words and events promotes it, she is able to give sound advice to parents. Dr. Casasola says that parents should talk to their babies as much as possible. "Research demonstrates that frequent communication with infants and toddlers is directly related to the amount of words babies learn."

Words

If you listen carefully to your baby's vocalizations, you will hear lots of sounds that seem like words or short phrases. Sometimes you will hear many sounds tied together that will make you think your baby is trying to tell you something important.

Materials
None

Behind the Scenes

While it may seem that baby development happens naturally, many forces foster each and every advance. What is interesting, reassuring, and wonderful is that most of the necessary parenting or caregiver support comes naturally. While babbling provides a natural inclination to babble back, specific babbles that start to resemble real words have their own way of encouraging adults to model with joy the real words they resemble.

How to Do It

1. Whenever you hear babbling that sounds like words, phrases, or general concepts, say the real words back to your baby.

2. For example, if you hear your baby say, "wa-wa," you might say, "Water. Do you want water?"

3. Do this as often as possible whenever you hear your baby make sounds or point at objects. Say the name of what your baby is pointing to, and describe it in as much detail as you can.

Research Roundup!

The website Parenting Literacy features an article by Dr. Joseph Lao, "Infant Language Development," which says that between ten and twelve months of age, infants begin to use what Dr. Lao calls "protowords." These are sounds that are similar to but are not quite words. Common examples are *mama*, *dada*, and *baba*. These words are different from repetitive babbling, which involves repeating sounds like *ba-ba-ba-ba-ba*. Protowords are shorter and typically one to two syllables. While it is clear that in repetitive babbling the infant is just producing sounds, these beginning words have more purpose, closely approximate speech, and generally correspond to something concrete such as mommy, daddy, or car and are used consistently to refer to the same person or object. Once these words begin to appear, they signify that infants are making a transition from prelinguistic to linguistic communication. The first real word is typically uttered between ten and thirteen months of age and tends to be a noun of special interest to the baby.

Touch Walk

Your baby will hear all kinds of words, but she is likely to remember best those that she actually experiences in some way. Touch plays a big role in this area of learning.

Materials
Objects to touch

Behind the Scenes
Touch is a wonderful learning mechanism, and that is why texture books and activities are recommended beginning at baby's earliest days.

Research Roundup!
In an article from UrbanChildInstitute.org titled "Enhancing Development Through the Sense of Touch," many benefits for infant development are enumerated. In general, "Infants who experience more physical contact with caregivers demonstrate increased mental development in the first six months of life," and "the improved cognitive development has been shown to last even after eight years." Taking the concept one step further, touch-based learning for the baby is positive too. The article recommends pairing rich language with interesting materials and textures for play, to encourage development of sensory, language, and vision skills.

Reading Time IV

Rhyming words have great appeal to babies. Knowing this, and that your baby now has new word skills, she will be better able to follow along with the rhymes you choose.

Materials
Book of rhymes, preferably large print

Behind the Scenes
This is the perfect time in your reading interactions to help your baby connect printed words with what you say. Reading familiar rhymes will be best for this process.

How to Do It

1. Take your baby around the house or outside and encourage her to touch different interesting items.

2. Every time you find one, describe it using texture words such as *hard, soft, rough, smooth, heavy, light,* and so on.

3. Inside you may want to describe objects such as towels, pillows, napkins, paper, plastic cups and cutlery, doorknobs, and books. Outside you might find grass, twigs, stones, trees, leaves, patio furniture, and so on.

4. Whenever you find an object of interest, you can also add full-body experiences. A soft bed or a hard floor are great examples of things that look and feel totally different.

How to Do It

1. Select a well-known rhyme in a book and recite it to your baby.

2. Many rhymes have hand motions that you may wish to do with your baby as well.

3. After she is familiar with the rhyme, read it as you point to the words.

According to "Nursery Rhymes: Not Just for Babies!" from Reading Rockets, nursery rhymes are important for young children as they grow because they help develop an ear for language. Both rhyme and rhythm help children hear the sounds and syllables in words, which help children learn to read!

The Alphabet Song

Everyone loves "The Alphabet Song." It is one of the first songs parents usually sing to their babies, and its simplicity can help your child begin to learn the alphabet.

Materials

Paper

Behind the Scenes

Parents love this song for its educational value, but few realize the importance of helping baby connect the visual letters with the sounds they are singing. Add sight and even touch to the sound part of singing this song. At this age, your baby won't understand the sumbols, but she will enjoy interacting with you.

Research Roundup!

"One of the most important concepts that children can learn, even during their first three years of life, is that the printed language can be used to accomplish many different goals," according to *Baby Power: A Guide for Families for Using Assistive Technology with Their Infants and Toddlers*, on www.floridahealth.gov. Another related concept is teaching awareness of the print-to-speech relationship.

How to Do It

1. Make a simple alphabet chart to go with the rhythm of the song. You can use this pattern as a guide for setting up the letters.

   ABCD
   EFG
   HIJK
   LMNOP
   QRS
   TUV
   WX
   Y and Z
   Now I know my A B Cs.
   Next time won't you sing
      with me?

2. Point to the letters and words as you sing the song.

3. When you finish singing the last line, hug your baby and say, "I love you," or any other proud words that will please your baby.

Self-Esteem Grows with Daily Recognition

If You're Happy and You Know It II

A major aspect of self-esteem development is helping your baby feel good inside and out. This song must have been designed especially for this purpose.

Materials

None

How to Do It

1. Sit opposite your baby in a comfortable position.

2. Be sure that you are connected in such a way that you can easily help your baby with the motions.

3. As your little one becomes familiar with this song, she will be able to do more of the movements by herself.

4. Here are the words, with the motions marked.

   If you're happy and you know it, clap your hands (Clap hands)
   If you're happy and you know it, clap your hands (Clap hands)
   If you're happy and you know it, then your face will surely show it
   If you're happy and you know it, clap your hands (Clap hands)

   If you're happy and you know it, stamp your feet (Stamp feet)
   If you're happy and you know it, stamp your feet (Stamp feet)
   If you're happy and you know it, then your face will surely show it
   If you're happy and you know it, stamp your feet (Stamp feet)

   If you're happy and you know it, pat your head (Pat head)
   If you're happy and you know it, pat your head (Pat head)
   If you're happy and you know it, then your face will surely show it
   If you're happy and you know it, pat your head (Pat head)

   If you're happy and you know it, do all three (Clap hands, stamp feet, pat head)
   If you're happy and you know it, do all three (Clap hands, stamp feet, pat head)
   If you're happy and you know it, your face will surely show it
   If you're happy and you know it, do all three (Clap hands, stamp feet, pat head)

Behind the Scenes

Talk about happy things, and you feel happy. Talk about sad ones, and you feel sad. This song combines happy words with vibrant motions to create a positive mood for your baby.

Research Roundup!

An article by Darcia Narvaez, PhD, "Where Are the Happy Babies?" discusses concern about baby happiness being overlooked in modern life. Dr. Narvaez notes that many babies she has recently seen "tended to look distracted, unhappy, dazed, and pretty uninterested in others. And their eyes didn't glow or communicate understanding." Dr. Narvaez found that the care babies received in the first year made the difference in baby happiness. "Caregiver care in the first years of life is *critical* for optimal brain and body development and for intellectual, social, and emotional intelligence." How caregivers interact with babies is most important, and treating them in a happy way is a big part of the process. "Babies need caregivers to teach their bodies and brains to stay calm so they can grow well."

Color Song

This song combines your baby's name with attention to what she is wearing. This combination builds self-awareness in a positive and nurturing way.

Materials

None

Behind the Scenes

Each part of this activity fits with enhancing growth. The clothing descriptions teach vocabulary, and the focus on colors is of direct interest to babies. Repeating her name in the context of pleasant music and singing may provide a feeling of acceptance and joy for your baby.

Research Roundup!

"Does Singing to Your Baby Really Work? The Science Behind Infant-Directed Singing" by Dr. Kimberly Sena Moore in *Psychology Today* says studies suggest that singing to an infant is a first language lesson that can prevent language problems later in life. Researchers looked at speaking in a sing-song manner, lullabies, and various play songs, and found that caregivers across cultures, whether through singing or speaking, helped elevate mood levels and increased the emotional bond between caregiver and infant. "Even if you

How to Do It

1. Sit either next to each other or in front of a mirror.

2. Before you begin singing, point out to your baby the clothes you are both wearing.

3. When you are singing, point to those items as they come up in the song.

4. Each stanza is the same except for the color and the clothes you select.

   Sally's wearing a red dress, red dress, red dress.
   Sally's wearing a red dress all day long.
   Sally's wearing yellow socks, yellow socks, yellow socks.
   Sally's wearing yellow socks all day long.

feel like you 'can't sing' or you are 'tone deaf,'" it does not matter to your baby. "Your baby loves your voice and feels connected to your way of singing."

Mommy's Purse

You may offer your baby a baby book, but she will want the one you have. You may take out a baby play mirror, but your little one will ask for the adult one. Basically, your baby likes the real thing. While you will often have to discourage your baby from touching your things, now you can let her see and touch some of your things under guided conditions.

Materials
Handbag
Safe items to explore, such as plastic baby keys; a clean, small change purse; or a small notepad of paper. Small baby toys that your baby particularly likes should work very well too

Behind the Scenes
Toys of today represent a new concept. Most are reproductions of items that exist in the real world. Stacking cups, similar to measuring cups, and nesting bowls, similar to measuring bowls, and more are descended from days when parents gave their children real items for play. It only makes sense that our reproductions will not be as exciting and enticing as "the real thing."

Research Roundup!
"Using Toys to Support Infant-Toddler Learning and Development" by Gabriel Guyton in *Young Children* talks about using both store-bought and home items for play. "Play is the mechanism by which children learn—how they experience their world, practice new skills, and internalize new ideas—and is therefore, the essential work of children. Many advertisements lead consumers to think that toys are better if they are expensive store-bought items. In reality, the best toys are selected based on their appropriateness for a child's age, development and interests." He offers some suggestions for toys made of homemade or readily available items—fabric, bottles, cardboard boxes, yarn, cooking pans, and pinecones. Babies and toddlers under two may enjoy exploring shoe boxes, cereal boxes, plastic bowls, cups, and paper bags filled with crumpled newspaper and taped shut.

How to Do It

1. Find safe and interesting items and place them in a purse for your baby to explore.

2. Let your baby reach into it and take out items one at a time.

3. As she plays with each one, you can tell her as much about it as you would like. Do not leave your baby alone with any of the items.

What's Inside the Box?

An empty tissue box is tailor-made for this activity. However, a shoe box or other similarly sized one would work well too.

Materials
Empty box
Small, safe items, such as a sponge, plastic spoon, crayon, paper cup, child's block, toy car, a small doll

Behind the Scenes
Because new items with descriptions capture your baby's attention at this time, this surprise box is likely to be a big hit. Colors, textures, and exploration will bring self-satisfaction to your baby.

How to Do It

1. Place small items inside your box of choice.

2. Select items that are not too small to be swallowed; that have interesting colors, shapes, or textures; and that would be easy for your baby to pick up.

3. Take turns picking an object.

4. Talk about and describe each item as it is picked.

Research Roundup!
"Self-Confidence Starts Early" according to UrbanChildInstitute.org. Early self-esteem building is important in growing children with high self-confidence who feel competent and capable. Children who lack it feel that they do not measure up, and this belief can eventually lead them to avoid challenges and new experiences. Self-esteem contributes to well-being by improving coping skills and providing a buffer against negative events and influences. Self-confidence is grounded in early experiences, and a baby's first social interactions are important. Remember the old saying, "It is not what you do; it is how you do it." Any toy that can be played with through loving interaction is the kind that helps contribute to high self-esteem.

Baby Hokey Pokey

This is a great way through song to introduce parts of the body and the concepts of *left* and *right*. The more you help your baby focus on her body, the higher her self-awareness and positive self-concept will become.

Materials
None

Behind the Scenes
While these concepts might seem a little advanced for this age, it is never too early to start simple repetitive songs, and the more repetitive the concepts, the more effective the learning.

How to Do It

1. If your baby has standing balance, hold her hands while she stands. Give her as much support as necessary. If not, you can also do this activity with your baby on your lap.

2. Begin to sing.

3. Move your baby's arms, legs, head, and body to match the words of the song.

   You put your left hand in.
   You put your left hand out.
   You put your left hand in
   And you shake it all about.
   You do the Hokey Pokey
   And you turn yourself around.

4. Repeat this stanza five times.

5. Each time, substitute the words "left hand" with one of these sets of words: "*right hand, left foot, right foot, head,*" and "*whole self.*"

Research Roundup!

Self-concept begins to develop at birth, according to "Self-Concept: Infants, Toddlers, and Preschoolers" on the website of Supporting Success for Children with Hearing Loss. "As the child grows into a toddler and preschooler, her ability to interact successfully with her environment promotes a healthy self-concept." During this time, important input is needed from responsive and supportive parents and caregivers. According to the website, by the end of the first year, babies have made beginning progress on their long journey ahead to "picture themselves as separate persons capable of thinking and acting for themselves." Helping children develop a positive self-concept is difficult, and "there is no easy, foolproof formula for accomplishing this." Here are some of the components that are part of the task: praising appropriately, respecting, accepting, investing time, setting reasonable goals, and evaluating your accomplishments realistically.

PART II

One Year to Two Years

As you continue your parenting adventure, some new principles will come into play. These principles will help you through this next stage, which is full of mobility and exploration. While you can begin using these now, you will be able to adapt them as your child grows. I developed a concept called *FREE* to help parents to effectively communicate with young children.

1. **Fair, firm, and positive.** Be fair by explaining to your toddler what you expect. Be firm as you require that behavior. Be positive all the time.

2. **Respond**. Always respond to your toddler's needs and sometimes to his wants. Explain time, money, and/or energy constraints as needed, even with little ones. It is good that they know there are reasons for your choices.

3. **Enriched learning environment**. Expose your toddler to as many new and educational experiences as possible.

4. **Enriched language environment**. Implement the *R*, *S*, and *T* of parenting. Read, sing, and talk to your toddler as much as you can.

With a year of parenting behind you, you probably have built up quite a lot of confidence. Let it show. The more you say what you mean and mean what you say to your toddler, the more effective you will be. You can do all of that in a loving manner. This is the time to begin setting boundaries and giving guidance and support.

5 Twelve to Eighteen Months

The ability to use a few words and understand many more opens up wide avenues of participation for your child. Your toddler will now be able to ask for items. You will see him follow simple directions and begin to understand simple stories. Give your little one crayons, and he will scribble; put out blocks or other similar objects, and your toddler will put them in different places.

You are likely to have great fun as you notice thought behind simple actions. Read, sing, and talk to your toddler as much as you can. All during the first year, your baby was absorbing the input you set up in his environment. Now you will see how that year has made a huge impact on your child's development.

Toddler Time Brings a New Level of Play

While your baby changed quickly before from month to month, progress now will take place over larger segments of time. What you will probably like most about these activities is that you can play them repeatedly, and your toddler will learn and grow from each experience. You and your little one will be able to focus on new and different parts of the activity each time.

Milestones of Development

- Uses trial-and-error approach
- Uses one object to touch another object
- Follows an object when it goes out of sight
- Uses an object purposefully
- Imitates body gestures
- Imitates new actions
- Imitates household activities
- Manipulates small objects
- Stacks two blocks or similar objects
- Begins to scribble
- Starts to throw objects
- Crawls up and down stairs
- Likes routines and rituals
- Follows simple directions
- Enjoys stories
- Helps with household tasks
- Enjoys sharing rhymes and songs
- Uses single words; has about a ten-word vocabulary
- Imitates words
- Uses inflections
- Makes one-word requests
- Identifies one facial part, usually the nose, and a few body parts

Cognitive Skills Grow through Purposeful Play

Toot Toot

Trains are very exciting to children of all ages. You can probably buy pull-toy trains, but making one could prove to be even more worthwhile due to the creativity of making the toy and the fun you will both experience by playing with a more freeform version.

Materials

Items to create a train, such as large hair rollers, empty spools of thread, large beads, small toy cars, and empty single-serving boxes, like those for cereal, juice, or raisins
Ribbon, string, yarn, or shoelaces 1 yard long

Behind the Scenes

Walking and talking are just starting and should be encouraged at every turn. Therefore, having a fun item to take along with you to different places makes perfect sense. Walking around allows your toddler to see the possibilities and freedom that pulling an item provides. He will probably enjoy making sounds or saying words that describe his excitement.

How to Do It

1. After you select your train car items, thread them together with a ribbon, string, or shoelaces, about a yard in length.

2. The game is yours. You and your toddler are free to pull your trains all around your house. Your destinations can go as far and wide as your imaginations allow.

3. As you play, talk about the sounds a train makes, and discuss the different parts that make up a train.

Research Roundup!

According to an article on WhatToExpect.com, "Best Toys for Toddlers," you will probably notice that playing is your toddler's job. As he focuses on "puzzles or play sets, trucks or teddies, blocks or books, he is like a little scientist at work." Being more mobile is a great advantage for getting to more places, and new manipulative skills provide new ways to help him gain control of the environment and, as the article asserts, "be the boss of his world (even when it's frustrating)." Therefore, when it comes to buying, borrowing, or making playthings, variety is key. Every kind of toy can teach something: cause and effect, communication, taking turns, eye-hand coordination, and even recognizing patterns. "The best playthings do many things at once and are open-ended enough to continue to fascinate your little explorer as she grows," the article says.

Housekeeping

Because pushing and pulling are of great interest to your toddler, it is a good idea to tie the play to a real housekeeping activity, such as sweeping. There are small broom and dustpan sets available for purchase, or you can take an old broom and cut the long handle down to child size.

Materials
Broom and dustpan

Behind the Scenes
Toddler time is "copy-you time" too. Take advantage of this interest. All early learning is programming for later learning, so do whatever you can to make these modeling experiences as positive and as inviting as possible.

How to Do It

1. Model a sweeping activity with your broom and dustpan set.

2. Encourage your toddler to sweep right along with you.

3. Talk to him and describe the process in detail as you sweep.

Research Roundup!
Your child is learning though imitation, according to "What Your Child Learns By Imitating You" by Chana Stiefel on parents.com. She quotes Lisa Nalven, a developmental and behavioral pediatrician, who says that as a result of copying adults during this time, one-year-olds can learn many skills, ranging from language to social abilities. Toddlers especially enjoy imitating activities such as sweeping and vacuuming. Try to model any of these behaviors as much as possible, because your little one will learn by imitating you.

Recycle Bin II

Pretend play for your toddler revolves around using items with purpose. With that goal in mind, the specific objects you choose for this activity are very important.

Materials

Things to pretend with, such as empty plastic bottles, foam meal trays, plastic plates, plastic covered containers, and so on

Behind the Scenes

Going beyond the describing you did before, this is the time to encourage your toddler's originality. If opening and closing is the action of choice, add whatever scenario you like. If your little one is interested in pretend drinking or eating, talk about different drinks or food that might go with your toddler's actions. "Up and down" and "in and out" might have been enough description when he was younger, but storylines are now much more fun and valuable for learning.

Research Roundup!

In the book *Your Baby & Child: From Birth to Age Five* by Penelope Leach, one-year-olds are focused on the concept of "play and learn." You can buy a host of different kinds of toys that address a particular skill, but your toddler is primarily thinking about how to use every toy or object given to him as a tool for learning. Children at this age want to learn about their world and acquire grown-up skills.

How to Do It

1. Set up pretend-play activities with your chosen materials.

2. Make sure that all objects you use are safe for play—no sharp edges or pieces so small that they could be swallowed.

3. Talk about the materials, using as much vocabulary as possible: "Oh, are you pretending to drink some cold water?"

What's Happening?

Day by day, your toddler is out in the world trying to figure out what's happening around him. Pushing and pulling and handling small items are all part of the exploratory play with this activity.

Materials

None

Behind the Scenes

Through situations of all kinds, toddlers accomplish their very determined goal of learning about the world. Basically they are out to explore and do not stop at very much. They experience what is wet and what is dry, what hurts, what can be lifted, what is for pushing, what is for pulling, what makes

How to Do It

1. Choose specific places to let your toddler explore. It might be under a chair, behind a couch, or in a closet.

2. Wherever you choose, oversee what is going on and check for general safety.

3. As your toddler explores, talk to him and ask him questions as he learns about what's around him.

things stop and what makes them go, and what makes some things hold together and what makes others fall apart.

Research Roundup!

In *Constructive Parenting,* my book on early learning, toddler play is discussed at length from the standpoint of cognitive development. During the whole first year, little ones start to find out what they can do alone and when they need help. They experiment by seeing, feeling, hearing, tasting, and smelling and also drop, throw, and make a mess to learn about life and, as a result, grow in cognitive skills. Providing varied experiences is one of the responsibilities for today's parents and caregivers. These include imitation, verbal stimulation, reading, and singing and also the knowledge that every challenging event leads to the child's wonder.

Following Directions

Your toddler can follow simple directions. If you take the idea of following directions and set it up as a game, you both can have great fun.

Materials

A pack of 4" x 6" index cards
Marker or crayon

Behind the Scenes

Your toddler will love following simple directions. Even though this game focuses on his understanding of what to do, it is your delight that will mean the most. Your little one learns, and you show happiness about his progress. That is the perfect combination.

Research Roundup!

Even if a young toddler is not talking much, he will be able to understand simple requests. The article "Teaching a Toddler to Follow Directions" by Nicole Caccavo Kear details research from Lise Eliot, PhD, author of *What's Going On in There? How the Brain and Mind Develop in the First Five Years of Life*, which explains that simple requests such as, "Please hand me your socks," can be followed first. Between eighteen and twenty-four months, a child can graduate to more complicated, multiple-step instructions such as, "Go to your room and bring me your teddy bear." Short-term memory is necessary for a toddler to carry out a two-step request.

How to Do It

1. Write a series of directions, one on each card, such as *under, next to, inside, behind, on top of, near,* and any other related concepts.

2. Take turns with your toddler picking a card.

3. Read the word and then make up sentences such as these to act out:

   - Sit *under* the table.
   - Go *next to* the plant.
   - Walk *behind* the door.

4. Be sure to take your turn as well, following a direction.

5. Keep to a set of three concepts to use over and over in different places. That way you will be sure to teach the position concept and also have the opportunity to add new vocabulary at the same time.

Motor Skills Soar with Small- and Large-Muscle Development

Stacking Up

Blocks are great for this activity. Any size your toddler can handle will work, and the brighter the color, the better.

Materials
Blocks

Behind the Scenes
Stacking blocks in groups of two is a great way to introduce stacking. Your toddler is likely to be attracted to brightly colored blocks and will enjoy this new ability to act on his environment in such a purposeful way.

Research Roundup!
"Ten Things Children Learn From Block Play" by Derry Koralek in *Young Children* details the many advances children can make from this fun play. While nearly all early childhood educators and many parents already think highly of block play for little ones, very few are aware of all the benefits such play provides. One year of age is an optimal time to start, as young children can experience some measure of early development in the following areas:

1. Problem solving
2. Imagination
3. Self-expression
4. Mathematics
5. Continuity and permanence
6. Creativity
7. Science
8. Self-esteem
9. Social and emotional growth

How to Do It

1. Take blocks two at a time and begin the fun.
2. First, put out one block.
3. Show your toddler how to put a second on top.
4. Set up another block and ask him to put another one on top.
5. Keep making more and more stacks of two. Help as much or as little as necessary.

Where Is It?

While hide-and-seek is the full-blown version of this game, this activity can serve as an introduction to that play. Use two paper or plastic cups, each the same size. Find a safe item for hiding under one of them, anything with a pleasant texture and not so small that it may be swallowed.

Materials

Two paper or plastic cups
Safe item to hide, such as a large paperclip, a small block, or a large eraser

Behind the Scenes

Your toddler has a couple of new skills that make this particular game both a challenge and really fun! First, your little one is ready to use a trial-and-error approach. And, your toddler now follows an object even when it goes out of sight. No longer accepting that the object is gone forever, his new idea is to go about finding it.

Research Roundup!

"Almost anything that gets your little one to explore items with his hands works for manipulative play," such as squeezing playdough and splashing in the tub, says Eliza Martinez in her article "Manipulative Play Activities for Toddlers" on OurEverydayLife.com. Bubbles, nesting and stacking toys, as well as large connecting blocks are other toys that work for this type of play. Not only is manipulative play fun, it is also beneficial for brain development as he learns about size, shape, and weight. Your toddler will build early math skills by sorting, making patterns, and following sequences. Manipulating small toys provides exposure to being able to compare and contrast them. Most important of all, manipulative play develops muscles in your toddler's hands, fingers, and arms.

How to Do It

1. Put the two matching cups upside down on a table and place a small item that can fit inside under one of them.

2. Ask your toddler, "Where is it?"

3. Have him pull up a cup to find it.

4. If he is correct, play again.

5. If he is not, ask him to turn over the second cup.

6. Keep hiding the object and having your child find it for as long as the two of you wish.

Paper Plate Scribbling

Your toddler loves to scribble. He should find it especially fun to scribble on the ribbed portion of a paper plate.

Materials

2 paper plates
Crayons

Behind the Scenes

While it may seem early to expose your baby to crayons, it is not. The fine-motor skill is there, and most important is that you, as your child's first teacher, are setting up a new activity with boundaries.

Research Roundup!

J.J. Beaty writes in "Early Writing and Scribbling" on education.com that scribbling is the first step in the process of writing development. While it is easy to disregard this early stage of writing, it is most helpful to foster this skill with your little one. "Scribbling is to writing what babbling is to speaking: an early stage of children's development," Beaty says. Scribbling provides an opportunity for your toddler to begin to notice what he is doing. As his hands and fingers become stronger, you will notice the increased control. In time, Beaty asserts, "scribbles will begin to evolve into shapes: circles, ovals, squares, and crosses, among others, one on top of the other." Joy will come from making scribbles that cover much of the paper, which will mark the beginning of the differentiation between pictures and writing scribbles.

How to Do It

1. Put two paper plates on a table, one for each of you.

2. With a shared set of crayons, scribble all over your plates, ribbed rims included. Be sure to put down extra paper below so that stray scribbles will not show up in unwanted places.

Sock Toss

Socks make safe, soft balls, perfect for throwing inside the house. Toddler-sized socks make the best balls for your little one.

Materials

5 to 10 pairs of toddler socks
5 to 10 pairs of adult socks

Behind the Scenes

Hard objects could break fragile items and disturb others. These soft balls are quiet and pleasant to use.

Research Roundup!

"Why Your Child Should Be Playing With Balls" by Stephanie Brown on VeryWell.com explains how throwing, catching, kicking, and dribbling play special roles in improving motor skills, eye-hand coordination, and timing. Little ones seem to like playing with balls right from the start; balls allow children to feel in control of something other than their own movements. You can introduce a ball to your

How to Do It

1. Keep the socks rolled into balls as you might find them in your dresser drawers.

2. Set up a laundry basket or large box on the floor between the two of you.

3. With all the balls in front of you, take turns throwing them into the basket.

4. Try throwing them from different lengths and from different angles. Have fun as you create different kinds of play.

child early and feel comfortable. While in play, your child will strengthen motor skills, and the play will familiarize him with his environment. Rolling a ball back and forth is a way to build a social bond between two people, and it is also a very introductory lesson to cause and effect. Toddlers will discover all that a ball can do: bounce, roll, and be kicked and dropped.

Going Up and Down

Always be there to support your toddler as he crawls up and down. Be sure to keep an eye on your little one as he moves in different directions.

Materials
Sofa or couch

Behind the Scenes
Movement builds muscles, and stronger muscles create more movement. People are generally happier and feel better when they can move. It is important to provide your toddler as many opportunities as possible for safe, exploratory actions.

How to Do It

1. Sit comfortably on your sofa or couch.

2. Help your toddler get up onto the couch and snuggle up with you, and then help him crawl back down.

Research Roundup!
According to Burton L. White in his book *The New First Three Years of Life,* one year of age is a time when much climbing takes place, and the skill should be quite well-developed by that time. He also points out that sofa climbing, including to the arms and back, is a popular destination for the experienced climber. He cautions to keep safety first and foremost on your mind and to take precautions for getting poisons and other hazardous substances and objects out of reach. Also, keep an eye out during sofa-climbing time to make sure it does not lead to other dangerous spots, such as on some tables and other chairs that could tip over. Any sofa-climbing activity that includes you makes a pleasant and productive way to encourage this skill.

Be Social and Have a Great Time Too!

Number Songs

Your toddler enjoys routines. Setting up a song routine is likely to be a big success. Basing it on numbers will be educational and fun.

Materials
None

Behind the Scenes

Repetition and familiarity form the basics of early learning, so having a ready supply of songs to repeat and enjoy together makes good sense. Singing songs to feature the first five numbers lays the foundation for learning numbers, and that is beneficial too.

How to Do It

1. Select a song for each of the numbers from one to five.

2. Try the ones suggested, or other selections you know for some of the numbers.

One

"Hickory Dickory Dock"
Hickory dickory dock.
The mouse ran up the clock.
The clock struck one,
The mouse ran down.
Hickory dickory dock.

Two

"Two Little Apples"
Two little apples up in a tree
Smiled at me.
So I shook the tree as hard as I
    could
And down came the apples.
Mmm, they were good.

Three

"Old King Cole"
Old King Cole was a merry old soul,
A merry old soul was he.
He called for his pipe,
And he called for his bowl,
And he called for his fiddlers three.

Four

"Four Little Pumpkins"
Four little pumpkins sitting on a fence.
Along came the wind and blew a
    pumpkin down.
Three little pumpkins sitting on a
    fence.
Along came the wind and blew a
    pumpkin down.
Two little pumpkins sitting on a fence.
Along came the wind and blew a
    pumpkin down.
One little pumpkin sitting on a fence.
Along came the wind,
But this one stayed up.

Five

> "Five Little Monkeys"
> Five little monkeys jumping on the
> bed
> One fell down and bumped his head.
> Mamma called the doctor,
> And the doctor said,
> "Keep those monkeys off of that bed."
>
> Four little monkeys jumping on the
> bed.
> One fell down and bumped his head.
> Mamma called the doctor,
> And the doctor said,
> "Keep those monkeys off of that bed."
>
> Three little monkeys jumping on the
> bed.
> One fell down and bumped his head.
> Mamma called the doctor,
> And the doctor said,
> "Keep those monkeys off of that bed."
>
> Two little monkeys jumping on the
> bed.
> One fell down and bumped his head.
> Mamma called the doctor,
> And the doctor said,
> "Keep those monkeys off of that bed."
>
> One little monkey jumping on the
> bed.
> He fell down and bumped his head.
> Mamma called the doctor,
> And the doctor said,
> "No more monkeys jumping on the
> bed."

Research Roundup!

Research points out the importance of purposefully and intentionally introducing mathematics to children at a very early age. Researchers focused on informal mathematical knowledge and the principle that it takes place slowly and through firsthand exploration. More than twenty years of research shows that fundamental math skills are the building blocks for future success.

- Young children naturally engage in math play as they grow and develop (Seo and Ginsburg, 2004).

- Children's block play in preschool has been linked to future success in middle and high school, predicting the number of math and honor courses taken, math grades, and math achievement scores (Wolfgang, Stannard, & Jones, 2001).

- Early math skills are a strong predictor of literacy skills (Duncan et al. 2007).

Bring Me a . . .

Your toddler can follow simple directions. Give him simple instructions to expand his learning.

Materials
None

Behind the Scenes
Simple directions are great because your toddler can be successful following them. There are also endless possibilities for your instructions available. You can use the words *please* and *thank you* with them, important words to use with your little one right from the start.

Research Roundup!
According to the American Academy of Pediatrics' guide *Caring for Your Baby and Young Child: Birth to Age 5*, your young toddler will suddenly be able to understand just about everything you say. You might question your perception but should be pleasantly surprised to find out that you are right. This major developmental leap is likely to naturally cause you to take steps such as using less baby talk and giving up any high-pitched singsong monologues. What you will probably do is start using a lot of simple words and short sentences. By being the best language model you can be, you will be helping him learn to talk with the least amount of confusion.

How to Do It

1. Give your toddler some simple directions.

2. Have fun together as you both see how well he carries them out.

3. Here are some suggestions:
   - Bring me the cup.
   - Drink from the cup.
   - Bring me a towel.
   - Put the towel on the chair.
   - Bring me the telephone.
   - Talk on the telephone.

4. Do not forget to say *please* before each request and *thank you* after each accomplishment.

Reading Time V

Routines lay the foundation for discipline. Setting up a reading routine can be an enjoyable part of this process. Before bed is a natural time to read together, but you may also want to include another time during the day in which you both are less tired and more relaxed.

Materials
A picture book
Large-print book
4" x 6" index cards
Marker or crayon

1. Read the picture book in such a way that it makes sense to your toddler.

2. Next, read a large-print book to your toddler.

3. Point to the words as you read them.

4. Try to read the same book over and over so that your toddler will become familiar with the words. In time, he will be able to participate more in the reading process by filling in words here and there.

5. End the routine by reading and acting out word cards. To make the cards, print the words *hop, jump*, and *clap* on index cards.

6. Add more words after your toddler becomes familiar with these.

7. Take turns picking a card and then acting it out.

Behind the Scenes

You cannot start too early making books a part of your child's life. Treat books with respect and expect your toddler to do so as well. Show him how to hold a book in its correct upright position, and teach him to never leave it on the floor. It is important to be consistent with what you require.

Research Roundup!

Stanford researcher Shirley Brice Heath found that children who were read to interactively became better readers. Heath studied adult practices of story reading to preschool children and found that when parents provided their children with children's books and read storybooks to them while communicating, students performed well in reading.

Now You Do It

Your toddler will enjoy imitating you in this activity. He will learn from you as well.

Materials

None

Behind the Scenes

An activity is only good if both you and your toddler enjoy it. Because imitation should be right up his alley, you two are likely to keep going with these activities for quite a while.

Research Roundup!

Imitation is a big part of the learning process at one year of age, according to the American Academy of Pediatrics' *Caring for Your Baby and Young Child: Birth to Age 5*. "Instead of just manipulating objects, as he did during his first year, he'll actually use a brush on his hair, babble into the phone, turn the steering wheel of his toy car, and push it back and forth."

How to Do It

1. Sit on the floor with your toddler.

2. Start the imitation process with sentences such as these:

   I clap my hands. Now you clap your hands.
   I pat my head. Now you pat your head.

3. After you have done several motions on the floor, get up and pretend to do some real household activities. Here are some examples:

   I sweep the floor. Now you sweep the floor.
   I dust the table. Now you dust the table.

4. Once you start with one or two actions, then make up some more. Have fun as you create.

Row, Row, Row Your Boat

This age-old song is pleasing to sing and can be turned into an exercise for your child's benefit. A song is good, but one with actions is more valuable in terms of the learning possibilities and the movement it provides.

Materials
None

Behind the Scenes
The words to this song on a symbolic level have a positive effect in their own right. Because you are a participant in this activity, you have the opportunity to act that out as you sing it.

Research Roundup!
The concept of belonging, widely recognized as a fundamental part of human development, is a key element in most early childhood curricula. Singing plays a big role in the development of the feeling of being accepted for children ages six months to two years, according to Amanda Niland, PhD. According to Dr. Niland's research, relationships between children and adults and among peers

How to Do It

1. On the floor or carpeted area, sit opposite your toddler close enough to hold hands.

2. As you both spread your feet apart, your toddler's feet will land somewhere near your thighs.

3. Hold hands and let your toddler pull you back and forth to the tune of "Row, Row, Row Your Boat."

4. Having him do the pulling will help build his muscle strength, as well.

showed strong evidence that singing plays a big part in building a sense of identity and belonging. "This research contributes to literature on the musical lives of infants and toddlers that supports the value of music, especially singing, in early childhood."

Enriching Language in New and Different Ways!

Puppet Talk

A small baby sock can become a puppet for your toddler, while a large adult sock can be one for you. Puppet talk has a way of encouraging toddler conversation that regular talking does not.

Materials

Adult and baby socks
Marker

Behind the Scenes

It is great to have conversations with your little one, but it can be hard to think of what to say. You can solve that problem with puppet play. Once you make your sock puppets and begin your pretend play conversations, you will be off to a great start! One scenario is likely to lead to another, and that can be great fun.

Research Roundup!

Puppets are a great way to focus attention due to the fact that they can stimulate the imagination of children of all ages, according to the article "Using Puppets in Child Care" on the website Extension.org. Using puppets provides an enjoyable way to teach new skills and concepts. Researchers have identified several areas of development on the toddler level:

How to Do It

1. Use a permanent marker and draw a happy face on each of your chosen socks.

2. Use the toe area to make the face and save the heel part for the lower part of the puppet's mouth.

3. For each one, place your fingers in the toe section and your thumb in the heel one.

4. Speak to each other with your puppets. Feel free to create your own special conversations.

5. You can even use socks without faces on them. They lend themselves to being puppets too.

- **Social skills**: Puppets can increase toddler communication and social skills by providing structured opportunities to interact.

- **Emotional development**: Puppets can support toddlers emotionally by giving them a "friend" to talk to or a way to talk to other children without having to speak directly to them.

- **Music appreciation**: Puppets can make music and creative movement more interesting and can teach toddlers the words and movements to new songs.

You Touch It, You Name It

Names for parts of the body hold high interest for your toddler. Clothing items stimulate language as well.

Behind the Scenes

This is a great time for you to get used to this fill-in-the-blanks type of language. Your toddler will get a lot of fun out of answering before you do. For those times that he does not know the correct response, you will be close behind with the right word for him to learn.

Research Roundup!

Young children are able to learn large groups of words at the same time, according to researchers Linda Smith and Chen Yu at Indiana University. The researchers' theory, which they explored with twelve- and fourteen-month-olds, shows that exposure to combinations of words and images instead of one word at a time made the children surprisingly successful at figuring out which word went with the correct picture. Different from the accumulated word theory in which toddlers were thought to be able to learn just one word at a time, these results support the idea to keep using as much descriptive language with toddlers as possible.

How to Do It

1. Choose a sentence that your toddler will like. Here are some examples:

   This is my . . . head.
   Here is my . . . hand.
   I like my . . . shirt. You might have another one that you like.

2. Point to a part of the body or a piece of clothing and say your sentence.

3. Hesitate before you fill in the correct word to give your toddler a chance to say the name first.

4. Encourage your toddler to imitate you as you play.

Private Spot

Pretend play usually brings about much new language. Making the pretend play in a private area gives it more of a mystique, and that adds to the effectiveness of the language stimulation.

How to Do It

1. Cover a small end table, card table, or chair with a blanket or sheet.

2. Put in the covered area whatever props you like.

   - If you have plastic cups, plates, and cutlery, you could call it a restaurant.
   - If you have dolls and doll furniture, you could call it a house.
   - If you have a play cash register and some food boxes or cans, you could call it a store.

3. Enjoy playing with your toddler as he discovers and explores the hidden items.

Materials

Small table
Blanket or sheet
Items to pretend with

Behind the Scenes

The principle of peekaboo is here again. Finding hidden objects is just plain fun no matter what age the child. With your young toddler, the emphasis of the play will be on naming the items and then discussing them. In time, more and more of the activity will be on the pretend aspect.

Research Roundup!

Anne Fernald and colleagues have found that children become more and more efficient in recognizing, understanding, and speaking new words across their second year. Rather than learning new words one at a time, children become better at recognizing the same words in more diverse contexts.

Mirror Fun II

A mirror provides a great stimulant to language development. The first mirror activity on page 25 was one that brought out sounds—gurgles, coos, and other responses. This one focuses on words.

Materials

Handheld or wall mirror

Behind the Scenes

A mirror goes hand in hand with language enrichment. From research we know that labeling is effective and that general language works well, and the mirror is good for both. There will be so many simple items to point out, such as hands, shirts, shoes, and more. There will be so much to talk about based on smiles, clapping, and all kinds of other actions and interactions.

Research Roundup!

Mirrors are a natural tool for getting a great look at people interacting, and they also provide important input related to self-identity, according to "Infant-Toddler Development with Daycare Mirrors" by Laurie Patsalides on BrightHubEducation. com. Patsalides says that mirrors are considered an effective tool to use in the social and self-awareness development of infants and toddlers, and language

How to Do It

1. Sit in front of a mirror with your toddler.

2. Listen for sounds.

3. If you hear something like "ah," you could point to your arm and say, "Arm."

4. If you hear, "Arm," you could point to your baby's arm and say, "Your arm."

5. If you hear something like, "My arm," you could say, "This is your arm."

6. The idea is to keep responding to the sounds and words you hear by taking them to a higher level. You will probably notice that this is quite a natural progression.

enrichment plays a big role in both of those areas. "Young children can also develop prereading skills from the use of mirrors by learning pronunciation, vocabulary, and the skill of identification."

Keeping Order

You can do this activity with any objects you have that come in large quantities.

Materials

Items that come in large quantities, such as children's blocks; large, colored paper clips; crayons; markers
Containers

Behind the Scenes

The older your toddler, the easier this activity will be. For this stage, starting simple is a good idea.

Research Roundup!

I designed a technique for stariting to keep order in *Baby and Toddler Learning Fun*. The method recommends that parents or caregivers make "shape seats," which can be used by young children to mark specific areas or play stations. This activity can inspire a toddler to sort and categorize in many different ways, which is so beneficial for his skills mastery.

How to Do It

1. Lay out your items in one area.

2. Set up appropriate containers in another.

3. Take turns putting an item in its proper container.

4. Keep playing until all the items are in the right places. You can start out with a few of each item and work up to larger numbers.

Build Self-Esteem with Child-Centered Fun

Where Are You?

Awareness of self is now being expanded to your home. When your child was younger and more attached to you, being in one or a few places in your house was adequate. Now that your little one is in a more independent state, being in other secure places is important too.

Materials

None

Behind the Scenes

In this case, changing rooms creates a playful way to help your toddler get to understand more about his home and feel good about where he lives. Naming the room will start the process, then noticing different objects and naming them spontaneously will be important too.

Research Roundup!

Though doctors and other professionals give us helpful information, some of the best insights come from parents. The book *I Love You Daddy Even More: More Thoughts from a Father* by Eric Granitur includes ideas on how to make home a comfortable place for your child.

- "Listen to classical music in your home as much as possible. Classical music really does soothe the soul. Playing classical music has made us, our daughter, our cats, and our home more tranquil." Any soothing music you enjoy will work to make your home a place of relaxation.

- Make your home inviting by surrounding your family with things that calm and please you.

- Bring as much sunlight as you can into your home, as it has therapeutic benefits.

- Keep your home as open and friendly to young children's movement as possible.

How to Do It

1. Start anywhere. Begin the play with, "Where are you?"

2. For whatever you hear, answer with something like, "Yes, you are in the living room." Expand your play by pointing out different objects and describing them.

3. Keep the play going for as long as you two want, and then move to another room. Continue with the same pattern in each room. Plan to spend two to five minutes in each room before moving to the next one.

Toddler Time

Because you spend so many hours during the day telling your toddler what to do and what not to do, he will enjoy this free-form activity. Giving your toddler your complete attention is all you have to do.

Materials

None

How to Do It

1. Go into any room in your house and sit down together.

2. Do what comes naturally and let your toddler take the lead. That's it!

Behind the Scenes

So much parenting advice comes in the form of directives. Many of the ideas are excellent and very worthwhile. However, one of the biggest and most important concepts of all is often left out: paying attention. Distractions today are major, and they really do interfere with giving your child the most important gift of all—your undivided attention. Nothing is more powerful and means more to your child at any age than being heard and understood.

Research Roundup!

"One of the most important things parents can do to make discipline strategies more effective is to build a positive relationship with their child," and the best way to do that is by spending quality time together, says Amy Morin in "Positive Attention Reduces Behavior Problems in Kids." Positive attention is a powerful force. It can, she says, create an environment where children become "more eager to please, more respectful, and are more affected by consequences." As recipients of parent attention, children reduce their own attention-seeking behaviors. Toddlers are more likely to display calmness, cooperativeness, and peace.

Roughhouse

With all the educational guidance that abounds, roughhousing is often left out, and it is very important to a child's development.

Materials

None

Behind the Scenes

Bonding is a valuable part of your parenting experience, with no age limit. As you know, you build your relationship with your child day by day, and every minute counts. While you can accomplish only so much through your ordinary calm activities, you can well imagine the power of this kind of more active and stimulating physical fun.

How to Do It

1. Lie on a bed with your toddler on top of you.

2. Gently bounce him in every direction.

3. The key to this fun and excitement is not to leave your toddler suspended in the air at any point. For his security, your toddler should always be touching you in some way.

Research Roundup!

"Play—especially active play, like roughhousing—makes kids smart, emotionally intelligent, lovable and likable, ethical, physically fit, and joyful," according to *The Art of Roughhousing: Good Old-Fashioned Horseplay and Why Every Kid Needs It* by Anthony T. DeBenedet, MD and Lawrence J. Cohen. While this type of play can make parents nervous, the writers find that "humans are hard-wired for roughhousing, so the body and mind are happy when we let it happen."

Blowing Bubbles

Bubbles are very appealing to toddlers. Introducing this kind of play can contribute to the "I can do it" feeling that is so important to self-esteem development.

Materials

Bubble solution with bubble blower

Behind the Scenes

At this very young stage, there are so few activities that your toddler can do all by himself. However, popping bubbles is perfect!

Research Roundup!

The Colorado Department of Education's website lists the benefits of blowing bubbles in "Bubbles and Toddlers," including:

- Aids in breathing control and the development of complex mouth movements that are both related to increasing language development

- Strengthens muscles related to gross motor skills development by stimulating crawling, walking, reaching, and climbing to catch and pop bubbles

- Teaches cause and effect by blowing into a wand and then seeing bubbles come out

The main perk for toddlers is the feeling of accomplishment that is intrinsic to the success of each bubble popped.

How to Do It

1. Use a bottle of bubble solution or make your own from a half cup of dishwashing detergent diluted with a little water.

2. If you do not have a plastic bottle blower from another bottle of bubbles, you can make a wand with a pipe cleaner.

3. Blow the bubbles and watch your toddler follow them around, popping them.

4. If your toddler seems up to it, show him how to blow bubbles as well.

5. **Be careful that he does not lick the liquid**.

6 Eighteen to Twenty-Four Months

Your older toddler can now participate well in many activities and will probably love jumping right into the action. She can begin to exert her influence on what is taking place around her. With the ability to walk up and down stairs, kick a ball, jump, and run, your child can now go far and wide. An expanded expressive and receptive vocabulary goes hand in hand with this stage, making your older toddler into quite a conversationalist. Open spaces will make life much more pleasant for both of you at this time. Your yard, a park, or any other play area that is free, fenced in, and protected will be great.

While you were giving frequent explanations before, now is the time to focus on guidelines, boundaries, and rules. This instructive position will be helpful for both of you. When you make your expectations clear before you embark on almost any activity, you will be helping your older toddler in many aspects. Being proactive will play a major role in helping your daily activities progress as smoothly as possible.

Your Older Toddler Likes Direction

Now is your opportunity to take charge. Before, you might have found yourself giving in to some expressed preferences, but now it is time for you to take over. Explain what the plans are, set your child up for success, and then do your best to carry them out. Because your older toddler looks more to you now for direction, be ready, willing, and able to give it.

Milestones of Development

- Uses an object to affect another object
- Climbs to get something
- Moves around an obstacle if necessary
- Acts and uses toys and objects in a functionally appropriate manner
- Imitates actions
- Uses words from memory
- Turns a knob
- Stacks about six blocks
- Uses a push or pull toy
- Kicks a ball
- Begins to run
- Walks up and down stairs
- Jumps
- Imitates others
- Engages in solitary play, such as coloring and building with blocks
- Plays simple games
- Attempts to put on clothes
- Plays parallel with other children or adults
- Imitates phrases
- Has a 50- to 300-word vocabulary
- Identifies parts of the body and face
- Follows directions
- Puts two words together

Cognitive Functioning Shows through Speaking and Understanding

Large Plastic Bottle Caps

This is a wonderful time to start your own large-sized bottle cap collection. Bottle caps come in all sizes and shapes, and some may have writing on them. For this activity, it is recommended that you select the large plastic ones that come in solid colors. *Large* in this case is defined as being too big to swallow.

Materials
Large, solid-colored bottle caps
Plastic container

Behind the Scenes
"Open-ended" is the key to all valuable early childhood learning activities. Once you provide appropriate materials, your older toddler will take it from there.

How to Do It

1. Place the bottle caps in a container for your toddler to explore.

2. Count them, stack them, sort them, and create some interesting designs together.

Toys that allow children to direct their own play and use their imagination, and those that "have the potential to be different every time they play with them" are ideal, says Dr. Dimitri Christakis, director at the Center for Children's Health at Seattle Children's Hospital, in "Toys that Encourage Creative Play" by Jennifer Donahue. Not only are these toys more engaging for young children, they are also more valuable for development.

Paper-Plate Puzzle

No need to buy a formal puzzle for this stage. A paper plate is fine.

Materials
Paper plates
Crayons

Behind the Scenes
Your toddler is still young. That means that you can make simple play toys, and she will enjoy them just as much, if not more, than complex ones.

Research Roundup!
From the start, little ones love to play with puzzles, due to the way they challenge their thinking and exercise their minds, according to Janice Davis in her article "Why are Puzzles So Important for Kids Learning?" This particular kind of stimulation makes puzzles an important educational learning tool for toddlers and older children. Puzzles made for toddlers help them develop visual spatial awareness and to better understand learning concepts and appropriate categories.

How to Do It

1. Encourage your toddler to color on a paper plate. The design belongs to her.

2. Cut the plate into two pieces. Any way you decide to divide it works.

3. Return it to your toddler to put the pieces back together and have her own puzzle fun.

4. Try another paper plate and turn that one into a three-piece puzzle. Help as much or as little as is necessary.

Ball Play

Ball play is likely to become more prominent with your older toddler. This is as good a time as any to start. Part of the intrigue is that a ball never does the same thing twice. There is no time limit and no official beginning and end for this activity.

Materials
Beach ball or 7" to 10" rubber or plastic ball

How to Do It

1. Start by standing opposite each other and rolling the ball back and forth to each other. Let the play develop from there.

Behind the Scenes

While ball play looks like a completely physical activity, much of it is actually a result of clear and important thinking. Rolling a ball with control at different speeds and in different directions are the exact parameters needed to get a ball where you want it to go. Skill is required with every roll, and learning takes place with each and every attempt.

Research Roundup!

"It is important to stress the value of opportunities to engage in activities such as running, hopping, dancing, and throwing to help the child build physical skills necessary for later in life" according to Kathy Gunner and colleagues in the *Journal of Pediatric Health Care*. When it comes to throwing, catching, and kicking a ball, there will be growth in eye-hand coordination. The key is finding safe places such as a park or backyard that is equipped for active play. Experiencing her physical world daily is what helps a child keep up flexibility, balance, and strength as well as heart health.

The World of Animals

Animals' actions and sounds have a great appeal to older toddlers. This play also offers different learning benefits.

Materials

Magazines
Scissors (adult use)
5" x 8" index cards
Glue stick (adult use)

Behind the Scenes

Baby animals and their cute pictures are exactly what little children like to look at. Adding movements and animal sounds makes almost any kind of animal card game or picture book an older toddler favorite.

Research Roundup!

The concept of pretend play is being studied more seriously by researchers. This type of play may connect with "the ability to get along socially in the world," according to "The Power of Pretending" by Beth Azar.

How to Do It

1. Cut out pictures of animals from magazines.

2. Paste them on the index cards.

3. Form a pile of these index cards and, with your toddler, take turns picking one.

4. Do what you can to imitate the animal. Move like the animal or imitate its sound, if possible.

5. If your older toddler has difficulty with her animal, help her as much as you can. Dogs, cats, lions, and elephants are good starters.

One-to-One

A small collection of large paper clips and a muffin tin or egg carton are needed for this activity. These clips are a good size and texture for your older toddler to handle, and those containers have compartments that are just the right size.

Materials
Large, multicolored paper clips
Muffin tin or egg carton

Behind the Scenes
One-to-one correspondence is a basic, gradually learned, and powerful skill. This game, which looks nothing like a mathematics activity and everything like pure fun, lays the groundwork for learning this concept in the future. Your toddler will likely have just the right level of fine-motor development to enjoy what you two are doing together.

Research Roundup!
"'Just One!' The Beginnings of One-to-One Correspondence" on WonderBaby.org explains a lot about the concept of numeracy and its relationship to counting. "Many people think of learning to count as the basic, beginning math skill to teach to children," according to the article, but "even before a child can learn to count, he or she must master the premath (numeracy) concept of one-to-one correspondence." That means that if you say, *one* to your toddler, she can count one object. Many children count by rote but have not yet learned what counting means. For this reason, learning to pick just one item is a foundational skill activity that can be a very effective part of this learning process.

How to Do It

1. You should both take a supply of multicolored paper clips.

2. Take turns putting one of your clips into an empty section in the muffin tin or egg carton.

3. The game is over when each section has a paper clip in it.

4. If you want to continue play, you can make the game over with two clips in each one.

5. If you have other ideas for safe objects to use like small blocks, checkers, or corks, that's fine too. Never leave your toddler unattended and always be on the lookout for items that could be swallowed.

Motor Progress Makes Playtime More Fun!

Build That Tower

Time to leave those piles of two behind. Now you and your toddler can become high-rise building partners.

Materials
Building blocks

Behind the Scenes

There is something in this game for both of you. You will love the new heights you two can reach, and believe it or not, your toddler will like the toppling part the best.

Research Roundup!

"Blocks represent a microcosm of life: your child can use them to construct his own understanding about how things work, and even how life works," according to the article "All About Blocks" on Scholastic.com. While block play is traditionally associated with fine-motor development, it turns out that it stimulates learning in other areas of development—cognitive, social-emotional, and language. There is even current research that shows it is related to later success with mathematics and numbers. Here are a few basics about block play and how it relates to areas of development:

How to Do It

1. Choose a block to go in the center between the two of you.

2. Take turns adding to the tower.

3. Strive for going up as high as six in a row.

- **Cognitive:** Much of this particular learning is about cause and effect. Filling and dumping, stacking, knocking down, and laying blocks side by side are all part of the picture. It also includes learning about sizes, comparing objects to make exact matches, and ordering.

- **Motor:** Awareness of how to hold on to the blocks, knowing how they feel, experiencing which are heavy and light, and being able to carry them around are all implicit in fine-motor skill development from this kind of play. Young children will also work on enhancing grasp with block play.

- **Social-emotional:** Growth comes from interacting with you in new and different ways.

- **Language:** Vocabulary increases naturally from enjoying time together.

Push It or Pull It

Push toys usually have a firm handle for pushing. Pull toys are totally different and have a loose string or ribbon for pulling.

Materials

Push and pull toys

Behind the Scenes

These toys are designed to delight your toddler in one way or another. Toy baby carriages or grocery carts give a purpose to the walk, stimulate pretend play, and, most important of all, lend just the right amount of support for a toddler who is growing in balance and

How to Do It

1. With your assorted push and pull toys, watch your toddler play. Your toddler will love this walking activity.

2. Be prepared for some spirited running as well.

coordination. Trains and cars that you pull have their own kind of intrigue. They encourage walking and sometimes running but do not provide any particular kind of gross-motor support.

Research Roundup!

"Why Push Toys Pay Off" on WhatToExpect.com says that young children love push toys, though these toys provide more than fun. First, they give support to babies who are not quite ready to stand or walk on their own. The pushing motion helps toddlers build strength, gain balance, and accrue confidence. Correspondingly, pull toys have their own way of boosting balance and coordination. Both push toys and pull toys make a contribution to the arena of imagination. Self-esteem can rise too when your little one finds herself "helping" you cut the grass, clean the carpet, or shop for groceries.

Ball Kicking

Recommended is a rubber ball or a beach ball. You may have another kind too, and outside is the best place to play.

Materials

10" rubber ball or 12" beach ball

Behind the Scenes

Just before being able to throw a ball comes kicking. While it can be done indoors, outside is best for all the running that appropriately goes with it. It is easy to see how beginning throwing could be next on the scene following this full-blown kicking activity.

Research Roundup!

Children learn "by watching someone else perform a task, imitating that person, and receiving positive reinforcement for their efforts," says David Geller, pediatrician, in "How Can I Teach My Child to Hit, Kick, and Catch a Ball?" According to this approach, you start by doing some kicks. You can progress to rolling the ball toward your child's foot and asking her to kick it. Then, even if the ball just touches her foot, you can reinforce what just happened by saying something like, "Nice kick." After you do this a few times, your little girl is likely to start on her own. When she kicks, you can give more praise. You will probably be surprised how quickly your toddler will learn what kicking means, and you will also likely enjoy that you have played a role in the process. Now that you have experienced the order, you can use this same method for what's next—throwing and catching a ball.

How to Do It

1. Use a rope to divide your yard into two parts.

2. You and your older toddler stand on opposite sides of the rope.

3. Kick the ball from your side over to hers.

4. Encourage her to kick it back to your side.

5. Have fun kicking the ball back and forth for as long as you both continue to want to play.

Up and Down

Real stairs are the best. However, if you do not have stairs, use a thick, sturdy book or two to be like one big step.

Materials

Large books (optional)

Behind the Scenes

Steps provide excellent exercise for your toddler, and they are good for you too. That means you can take advantage of this fun activity by sharing it.

Research Roundup!

People who climb stairs on a regular basis are in better shape and have higher aerobic capacity, according to Duke University Human Resources. Climbing stairs can help build healthy bones, muscles, and joints.

Jack Be Nimble

Knowing that your older toddler enjoys jumping is great information for you. If you enhance it with a fun rhyme, you will support motor development and also get the benefit of some memory training.

Materials

Unlit, wide, low candle

Behind the Scenes

It is interesting to note how many childhood rhymes and songs support learning early skills and concepts. They also have a way of keeping parent and child happy at the same time.

Research Roundup!

As part of a series of articles on Infant and Toddler Forum on physical activity for children, "Physical Activity in Early Childhood: Setting the Stage for Lifelong Healthy Habits" explains how important physical activity is to many aspects of child health and development. Surprisingly, even for young children, "a lack of physical activity is a risk factor for many health problems such as high blood pressure, weight gain, excess body fat, bad cholesterol, respiratory difficulties, cardiovascular diseases, and bone health problems." Moreover, the health benefits extend well beyond physical health to all areas of development—cognitive, motor, social-emotional, language, and self-esteem. Early childhood is also a

How to Do It

1. Start either at the bottom of real stairs or beside your homemade thick-book stairs. Hold your toddler by the hand and help her walk up.

2. Turn around and help her go down.

3. You might want to continue your activity with this chant:

   Here we go up, up, up.
   Now we go down, down,
   * down.*

4. Repeat the activity for as long as you both continue to enjoy it.

critical time for establishing healthy behaviors and patterns that carry over into later childhood, adolescence, and adulthood.

Social Fun Is Valuable in Every Way!

Tap, Tap, Tap

Tapping patterns is valuable all on its own. However, it is also a terrific activity for becoming aware of syllables, which is related to speech development.

How to Do It

1. Sit opposite your toddler at a table.

2. Tell your child to tap exactly the way you do, right after you.

3. Start this imitation game by tapping once. Encourage your child to tap once.

4. Next, tap twice, and then three times.

5. If this tapping activity goes well, switch to taps you can turn into repeating patterns. Here are some examples you can use three times each:

   Long, short, short
   Short, short, long
   Long, short, long

6. You can also do a pattern with words such as "ap-ple-sauce" or your "ol-der-tod-dler's-name."

7. You also might want to tell your child to tap for you, and then you can imitate that pattern as well.

8. Have fun tapping and imitating each other for as long as you two wish to continue.

Materials
None

Behind the Scenes
Share this activity with any speech therapist, and you will get accolades. Syllables and being aware of them form the building blocks of clear speech.

Research Roundup!
In my book *Constructive Parenting*, there is a section on language development activities for toddlers that suggests activities for enhancing toddler speech. During this year from one to two, you will hear your toddler's first words and then many more. While this might sound amazing, your

child's vocabulary will advance from about fifty words to about 300. Before, you were focusing on saying words and letters. Now it's time to begin using phrases and sentences as the basis of your communication. One very simple way to do this is through repetition. When you hear a word or a simple phrase that is not said clearly, repeat it back. Such repeating will help your toddler to hear it better. As you know, many parents have a tendency to correct their toddlers, and their little ones usually show some kind of resistance to that.

Playing Alone

Being able to play alone is a great skill to begin to foster. While it sounds like the opposite of a component of social behavior, in reality it is an important building block.

Materials
Tote bag
Items to fill bag: durable board books, coloring pad with crayons and stickers, playdough, small toy cars, dolls, and some special favorite toys without pieces

Behind the Scenes
Playing alone probably happens from time to time or maybe even often. What is different about this activity is that it has parameters, with specific guidelines that work like boundaries, and those are the exact conditions that exist when play is with others. Another obvious perk is that this bag is mobile, and you can take it with you when you are going to a place where he will need to keep busy.

Research Roundup!
In the book *Your Baby & Child: From Birth to Age Five,* there is guidance about play that focuses on giving your toddler freedom to enjoy toys and other safe household items without too much supervision. Author Penelope Leach

How to Do It

1. Set up a "play-alone" tote bag.

2. Fill the bag with play items that interest your older toddler.

3. Change the items at the beginning of every month.

4. Give the tote bag to your older toddler.

5. Set a timer for ten minutes.

6. Explain to him that he can play with the bag of toys until the timer rings.

7. At the end of the ten minutes, you can both decide together if you should reset the timer for another ten minutes or not.

recommends providing basics such as "space, equipment, time, and companionship" but to leave the development of your child's thinking to himself. "Your child is a scientist and inventor," she says, and needs to discover and explore things himself. Your job is to make sure he has "a laboratory, research facilities, and an assistant when he needs one." Within the limits of safety and acceptable behavior, what he actually does with his play materials is up to him. Although her advice differs from the world of directed play, these guidelines are not meant to replace teaching proper ways to handle materials or to give guidance anywhere and everywhere along the learning process. Leach says, "You can help by showing him that his farm animals can ride in his truck and his blocks make stables," and you are encouraged to have an "odds and ends" box for him to find materials such as leftover packaging paper, scraps of cloth, cardboard tubes, plastic jars, and so forth.

Hide-and-Seek

This game is an advanced form of peekaboo. Hiding objects and even hiding yourselves will be great fun for your older toddler.

Materials
Object to hide: ball, shoe, book, pencil, napkin, etc.

Behind the Scenes
Surprise is one of the major characteristics of an excellent toy or game. No child or adult outgrows enjoying this concept.

Research Roundup!
According to my book *Constructive Parenting,* there is an important concept called "play value." I explain, "The best toy in the world is of no value if nobody wants to play with it." Discounting how grand it could look or how expensive it could be, without play value to attract play, the toy will go unused. These are the four play-value attributes:

- Interesting to see

- Exciting to touch

- Creates interaction

- Has surprise

How to Do It

1. One at a time, hide an object in the same room or in another room.

2. After it is hidden with a small part of it showing, ask your older toddler to find it.

3. You can offer hints about direction as she looks about the room.

4. Another idea is to hide a kitchen timer or a music box. For those objects, you can keep them completely covered and allow their sounds to provide the necessary clues.

5. A popular variation of this game is to hide yourself from your older toddler or have your older toddler hide from you.

Toys that have these qualities are usually the simplest. Blocks, for example, whether in colors, natural wood, or some other material, are always interesting to see and exciting to touch. In addition, they are fine for playing alone or interacting with others. Surprise is built right in. What will your child make? Nobody knows until she makes it!

Parent Clothes

Dressing up in parent clothes will be great fun for your toddler. Besides the straightforward practice for your little one, you are both able to enjoy this activity without the pressure of appropriate dress or meeting any particular deadlines.

Materials
Clothes for dress-up

Behind the Scenes
Your toddler will especially like your big items because they are big. How funny it will be for both of you to see your regular shirt drape over your child. Whatever it looks like, you can be sure that pretend play might not be far behind.

Research Roundup!
"Teaching Your Child How to Get Dressed" on the Raising Children website offers practical ideas for this exciting, yet sometimes trying, stage of development. While you may be thinking about starting to involve your child later, you can also lay the groundwork earlier and then work into it over a few years' time.

Learning to get dressed is more than just putting on or taking off clothes. It provides practice for many skills in all areas of development.

- **Cognitive**: remembering what pieces of clothing go on first and even by learning to dress for different occasions and varied weather conditions

- **Fine motor:** buttoning and zipping

- **Gross motor:** balancing to pull on a pair of pants

- **Social-emotional:** enjoying productive time together

- **Language:** saying the names of types of clothes, colors, and sizes

- **Self-esteem:** "I can do it by myself" successes

How to Do It

1. Select some of your clothes that you do not mind your older toddler wearing.

2. Have fun telling her what to put on over her clothes.

3. Help with the dressing process as much as is necessary.

Playing Together

Older toddlers will enjoy playing together. However, while they will be in the same place at the same time, they will in essence be playing by themselves. Such play is called *parallel play.*

Materials

2 or 3 bins of toys

Behind the Scenes

While we may think of toys as being limited to store-bought items, little ones can turn almost anything into a toy. The biggest responsibility you have related to play is to monitor safety—by selecting the particular objects and also watching the behavior of the children, one to another.

Research Roundup!

Pretend play is very important to a child's healthy development, according to NAEYC. A position paper from the organization says, "dramatic play produces documented cognitive, social, and emotional benefits." A clinical report on the subject for the American Association of Pediatrics finds that play is so vital to healthy development that "it has been recognized by the United Nations High Commission for Human Rights as a right for every child," and many of those benefits come from pretend play. Adult interactions with young children are vital to this play, according to Deborah J. Leong and Elena Bodrova, writing in NAEYC's *Young Children.* "Without adult support, the play of many children is destined to never reach . . . fully developed status. Teaching children to play has to be as intentional." This play, they say, can grow a child's "social skills, emerging mathematical ability, mastery of early literacy concepts, and self-regulation."

How to Do It

1. Set up the bins with play items in them. Here are some examples:

   - Store play—Empty boxes, empty plastic containers, a toy cash register, and other items that remind you of a store

   - Cooking play—Plastic dishes, cups, cutlery, bowls, measuring cups, measuring spoons, spatula, wooden spoon, scoops, and other appropriate things from your kitchen

   - Dress-up—Old clothes, jewelry, pocketbooks, and any other accessories that you do not need anymore

2. Take out one crate at a time.

3. Model some pretend play.

4. Encourage the older toddlers to play together with the selected items.

5. Babies, toddlers, and children of different ages can play too. They will all use the play materials in different ways.

Language Expands Daily!

Cookie-Cutter Shapes

You will need a set of cookie cutters, a pack of index cards, and a pencil or crayon for this activity. Playdough cutters can be used too.

How to Do It

1. Trace a cookie-cutter shape onto an index card.

2. Set out three cookie cutters in front of your child. One cookie cutter should be the match for the index card.

3. Give your shape to your older toddler to match it to the cookie cutter.

4. After she matches it, tell her to say, "A match!"

5. Take another index card and trace another cookie-cutter shape.

6. Play the game again.

7. Repeat the whole process with three more cards so that you have five shapes altogether. Then set up different kinds of matching games. Here are some suggestions:

   - Match one shape to one card.
   - Match two shapes to two cards.
   - Match three shapes to three cards.
   - Match four shapes to four cards.
   - Match five shapes to five cards.
   - Place the shapes in a cup. Then take turns with your older toddler picking a shape and matching it to the correct card.

8. After each turn you or your toddler take, remember to say, "A match!"

Materials

Cookie cutters
4" x 6" index cards
Pencil or crayon

Behind the Scenes

This active matching game has the opportunity for lots of word fun. While you two may not notice it, there will be vocabulary for all different shapes and the chance to say numbers.

Research Roundup!

"Just as young children need nourishing food to build physical strength, they also need linguistic nutrition for optimal development of language and cognitive abilities," says Bjorn Carey in "Talking Directly to Toddlers Strengthens Their Language Skills" on news.stanford.edu. Researchers at Stanford University asked mothers to record their children in their everyday home environments, using special equipment. While the whole group tested was from a low-income population, some of the mothers used more language with their toddlers than others. Those children who were exposed to the higher quality and quantity of language when they were toddlers were the ones who had significantly larger vocabularies.

Category Collections

Exposure to print provides valuable reading exposure. This activity limits the printed words to two at a time, making their appearance simple and meaningful.

Materials
File folder with 2 pockets
4" x 6" index cards
Tape or glue stick
Magazines

Behind the Scenes
While your intent here is the introduction of a sorting activity, the addition of print gives it a reading dimension. Toddlers, who hear much speech during their day but have little opportunity to connect it with corresponding print, now have the chance.

Research Roundup!
While often overlooked, sorting plays a positive role in toddler learning, according to Sylvia Cochran on the Bright Hub Education website. Specific activities that focus on sorting provide quiet play but also teach at the same time. These activities for toddlers prepare them for the development of organizational skills and also serve as an introduction to classification. According to Cochran, educators credit sorting as a way to lay the groundwork for "future coursework and success in mathematics, music, chemistry, physics, and also biology—all fields that rely heavily on categorization."

How to Do It

Your older toddler is capable of following directions. Moreover, she is likely to enjoy doing it.

Materials

Empty tissue box

Items to fill box: plastic spoon, plastic cup, pencil, small doll, small toy car, sponge, keychain, children's block, a business card

Behind the Scenes

Children (and adults too) exhibit knowledge of speech they can understand on a much higher level than words they can use to express themselves. Therefore, giving your toddler easy directions with simple sentences using vocabulary that is above her level of everyday language should work just fine and truly end up being a fun game.

Research Roundup!

There is a well-established game for toddlers called The Directions Game. Here is how I described it in my book *Baby and Toddler Learning Fun*: On 4" x 6" index cards, write simple directions, one sentence per card. Then take turns picking a card and following the direction. Keep the sentence to three or four words." Here are some popular directions: Close the door. Tie your shoe. Clap your hands. Jump three times. Walk around the table. Point to the words when giving the direction to use the print and verbal word connection as an effective prereading skill. Toddlers usually enjoy following directions that are active.

> ### How to Do It
>
> 1. Fill the box with simple household items.
>
> 2. Take turns picking an object.
>
> 3. For each one, give your toddler a short direction. Here are some examples:
>
>   - Put the spoon in the cup.
>   - Lay the pencil over the paper.
>   - Place the doll on the bed.

I Like . . .

The more personalized reading books you make, the better. A 4" x 6" photo album is the recommended size for making this book. Both photos and index cards conveniently come in the 4" x 6" size.

Materials

4" x 6" photo album or index cards

Behind the Scenes

Children's books are amazing these days. They are attractive, and many are written by accomplished authors. Buying books and borrowing books from the library are both sound practices. However, no books can compete with those you make with photos of your child and your own annotations that go with them. "*I Like* . . . is a book designed to create a positive attitude, and that makes it even better.

Research Roundup!

In my book *Parent Involvement Begins at Birth*, there is information about making a family book. "A parent can expand the picture concept to a photo-album family book. In this toy, the child will see more pictures and more corresponding words." Preparing a book like this, which is likely to be repeated often, can lay the foundation for later learning to read these particular family members' names. "This book also teaches the concept of family by showing that only those in the family can be in this book, and family can be whatever the parent wants it to be—from strictly traditional to any variation of nontraditional, including dogs, cats, other pets, and even very close friends."

Please and Thank You

There are so many times you will be asking your child to do things. This activity will give you practice at respecting your older toddler with the word *please* and appreciating her with the words *thank you*. The best way to teach your child to say *please* and *thank you* is to use those terms when speaking to her.

How to Do It

1. Make a book with the title "*I Like . . .*"

2. On each right-hand page, place a photo of your older toddler doing something she likes.

3. On each left-hand page, write a simple sentence describing the activity. Here are some examples:

   - I like to swim.
   - I like to read.
   - I like to play.

How to Do It

1. Line up about five interesting items on a table.

2. Begin the activity with sentences like these:

   - Please bring me the cup. Thank you very much.
   - Please bring me the toy car. Thank you very much.
   - Please bring me the napkin. Thank you very much.

3. If your child brings the wrong item, say something like, "That is a sponge. Please bring me the napkin."

4. Avoid using the word *no* during this game. If your child is not getting most of them right and not enjoying the game, discontinue the activity.

Materials

Items to line up, such as a toothbrush, toothpaste, unbreakable cup, spoon, napkin, small doll, small toy car, sponge, and so on

Behind the Scenes

This game serves to teach your child basic manners. She will also appreciate the respect you are showing as you use courteous words with her.

Research Roundup!

According to the Dr. Sears website, teaching respect begins early. Parents are advised to:

1. expect respect.

2. teach politeness early, using terms such as *please* and *thank you* often.

3. model good manners. Children learn so much from modeling, so children will naturally follow a parent's behavior.

4. open requests by using your child's name, and expect them to do this as well.

5. practice inclusion. Including your child in social settings will grow her social skills.

6. forcing manners can be ineffective, so try not to correct your child often.

7. when you do need to correct behavior, do so politely.

Self-Esteem Shows with Child-Centered Play!

Look What I Can Do

Whenever your older toddler realizes she can do something, she will feel very good about it. The more you can help your little one realize her capability, the better it will be for her growth.

1. Write each of the following sentences on a separate index card.

2. Pick each card separately.

3. For each one, read the card and then demonstrate the simple action.

4. After you take your turn, encourage your toddler to "read" the sentence with you and then do the action on her own.

- I can walk.
- I can run.
- I can jump.
- I can clap.
- I can hug you.
- I can wave *hi.*
- I can sit on a chair.
- I can touch my nose.
- I can turn a doorknob.
- I can touch my toes.

5. Be as creative as you both like.

Materials

4" x 6" index cards

Crayon or marker

Behind the Scenes

The repeated word in each sentence is *can*. This empowering word has a direct, positive effect on self-esteem development.

Research Roundup!

Words can literally change your brain, according to Andrew Newberg, MD, and Mark Robert Waldman in the book *Words Can Change Your Brain*. The researchers state that a single word has the power to influence the expression of genes. Words such as *peace* and *love* can strengthen areas in our frontal lobes and promote positive functioning, while some words can increase motivation and build resiliency. Conversely, they say that there is hostile language that can have an equally dramatic negative effect.

Name Puzzle

Your child's favorite word is her name. This activity will visually grow her awareness of her name.

Materials

4" x 6" index cards

Crayon or marker

Behind the Scenes

Repetition and familiarity play the two biggest roles in learning for little ones. Repeating this puzzle activity with your child will build great familiarity with the order of the letters of her name and with the way her name looks.

Research Roundup!

In my book *Baby and Toddler Learning Fun,* there is an activity that promotes self-awareness through making a book with family member pictures in it. The purpose of the book is to teach the toddler who the family members are and how she is a part of them. However, because of the size of the family, it is difficult to accomplish the learning right away; what is needed is seeing the pictures over and over with their name labels repeated. At first the idea is for the parent to do all the reading. As the toddler learns more names, she will be able to recognize the people in the photos. Promoting the repetition will help accomplish this learning task, and the personal nature will make it more special to your little one.

How to Do It

1. Write out the letters of your toddler's name, one letter per card. If your toddler's name is Sarah, for example, write each of the five letters on a different card.

2. With your child, put the letters together to spell her name correctly.

3. When you first begin to play, focus on the correct spelling.

4. As your toddler gets used to it, have her participate as much as possible in putting the letters of her name in order.

Dancing Time

Your older toddler will love to have the opportunity to dance. There is music available that is designed for babies, but almost any kind with clear beats and rhythms will work.

Materials
A music player

Behind the Scenes
Because movement should be a big part of your older toddler's life, dance is a natural inclusion. While any walking, running, and jumping are good, dance will help to give boundaries and direction to your toddler's mobility, characteristics that will promote a feeling of accomplishment at the same time.

Research Roundup!
"Standards for Dance in Early Childhood" on NDEO.org highlights the value of dance for little ones. Most important is that it "embodies one of our most primal relationships to the universe. It is pre-verbal, beginning before words can be formed . . . innate in children before they possess command over language. . . . Children move naturally." There is evidence that children learn movement patterns in a similar way to how they learn language, and just as with evidence of speaking and writing, these accomplishments bring great pride.

How to Do It

1. Turn on the music and dance.

2. You can take turns or dance together. There are no rules for this activity. The only suggestion is to try to encourage your older toddler to keep the beat and rhythm as much as possible.

Dress the Parent

As your toddler is learning to dress herself, she can get excellent practice by dressing you. There's no pressure or time limit with this activity, just the opportunity to work on fine motor skills.

Materials
Adult clothing, such as a jacket, hat, gloves, scarf, socks, or shoes

Behind the Scenes
Even the smallest accomplishment on your "big" body will feel wonderful to your toddler. While you likely think about interacting with your little one usually in some kind of playful way, here you have the opportunity to do something real, and your older toddler will really like that.

How to Do It

1. Take out some outerwear clothing that your older toddler can easily help you put on, such as socks or a jacket.

2. Allow your older toddler to do as much of the dressing by herself as possible.

3. Once she's finished, thank her and tell her she's done a wonderful job.

Research Roundup!

Researchers David Grissmer and colleagues emphasize the importance of advanced fine-motor skills for school readiness. While so many other aspects of toddler and preschool learning focus on academic concepts, this research shows that "motor skills are an additional predictor of later achievement." Stronger motor skills early in life strengthen the neural connections that assist children in many academic tasks. The more motor skills children develop, the more experiences they are able to have, and, in turn, those experiences make them better prepared for later cognitive academic success.

Hand Tracing

As she approaches a stage of new identity separate from her parents, your older toddler will especially appreciate any activity that focuses on her body. Hands are a great way to begin.

Materials

Pencil or crayon
Sheet of white paper

Behind the Scenes

Paying attention to your child helps to build her self-esteem. Focusing on something specific, such as her hands, strengthens your efforts in growing her self-awareness; inviting her participation in the process enhances your effectiveness even further. While one might normally do an activity like this without focus on the words, writing them, pointing to them, and reading them play a big role in a process called *print awareness*, or the basic understanding that words have meaning.

> ## How to Do It
>
> 1. Trace your little one's hands.
>
> 2. Write *Left* above the left-hand tracing and *Right* above the right-hand one.
>
> 3. Across the top, write your toddler's name.
>
> 4. Give her a crayon to scribble on the paper.

Research Roundup!

According to the Texas Education Agency, "Children with print awareness understand that written language is related to oral language." While beginning reading education usually starts with an approach to the mechanics of word recognition and phonics, the concept of print awareness is very important to future reading success and can be introduced in many different ways on the toddler level. Adults can promote it with little ones by working to point out letters, words, and other features of print and reading to them often. Turning pages of books, finding the top and bottom of the page, and identifying the front and back cover are all excellent activities that adults can practice with toddlers. Children who have this awareness know that writing on a page represents words, and it is this knowledge that gives them a jump start on learning to read.

PART III

Two Years to Three Years

This book is full of all kinds of parenting advice. However, there is one underlying characteristic that is responsible for making everything go right, and that is love. If you love your child, you will know what's best for your child. While that is wonderful news and sounds like the solution to all problems, there is more to it.

Because every parent, child, family, and community is different, there are specifics to consider at every place and turn, and no one formula to follow. However, if there were, it would go something like this: Learn as much as you can every day, and then do your best to guide your child. You are the one who makes the positive difference in your child's life. All the little things that you do add up to show your deep care and love for your child. Every day, you impact the life of your child in your own special way. No one can do it better, and there is not one moment to waste as you support your child's growth.

This is a very important time to remember your expertise as guide, supporter, and nurturer of your child. You have the strongest power and ability to love him. Use your skills as you work with other professionals. If your child is in a child care program for all or part of each day, remember that the caregiver is helping you. If your child is in any kind of therapy program, the therapist can assist your child and even teach you important techniques. Ultimately, you should be the one to take charge. If a grandparent, aunt, uncle, cousin, or friend oversteps boundaries by telling you what to do with your child, accept the suggestion but be comfortable making your own decisions.

7 Twenty-Four to Thirty Months

While previously your older toddler was busy touching everything, as a two-year-old, he is more selective. He wants to know how everything works. That makes him more determined and harder to manage. This is also a time you will notice how attached your little one may be to a particular doll, stuffed animal, or blanket.

You will probably find it very exciting that your child is beginning to understand a lot more. He should also exhibit a major increase in attention span, and that will open up many more learning opportunities, lots of play possibilities, and more time for reading. You are your child's first and most important teacher, so try to use this stage to begin the lifelong teaching process with your child.

Terrific Twos: Your Little Explorer Is Here!

This third year starts a transition into the beginning stages of adult-like functioning. Children at this stage are ready to do many of the things that adults do and want to be with them as much as possible. By age three, all meals should be on an adult schedule, and using the bathroom should be routine. Walking, talking, running, jumping, and more will be more fully formed. This is the ultimate stage of those all-important first three foundation years of life. Enjoy this very special time.

Milestones of Development

- Begins understanding size
- Begins understanding spatial relations
- Begins awareness of quantity
- Begins awareness of similarities
- Begins to sort
- Begins to show hand dominance
- Begins to throw
- Is possessive of objects and loved ones
- Resists change and likes routines
- Begins pretend play

- Begins to make words plural by adding an *s*
- Requests help by using sentences such as, "I want juice."
- Identifies objects by description
- Understands categories such as size, shape, and color
- Names some objects in a picture and some people
- Follows simple directions

Cognitive Development Grows by Leaps and Bounds

Car Play

Zoom, *vroom*, and *whoosh*. These are probably all words you hear connected with car play. Now is the time to encourage that play into a more meaningful and instructive situation.

Materials
Toy cars
2 ribbons or masking tape

Behind the Scenes
Reality is the goal for all teaching now. Observe what your child does naturally, and extend whatever concepts seem feasible. You might use this opportunity to teach the rules of the road and ways to be careful around traffic. There is much information children need to learn about drivers, passengers, and pedestrians.

Research Roundup!
"Often, injuries happen because parents are not aware of what their children can do," according to the American Academy of Pediatrics. Children learn fast, and jumping, running, riding a tricycle, and using tools all present their own hazards. Playing and exploring also take a lot of your

How to Do It

1. Set up a pretend roadway with the two pieces of ribbon or with masking tape. You can also wind two parallel pieces of yarn throughout the room or draw an attractive road system on a large piece of paper.

2. However you choose to set your road up, enjoy pretend travel with your child. Participating in the play is what will make it meaningful, expand your child's horizons, and introduce new and interesting vocabulary.

two-year-old's full energy and attention. Even if you think your child knows about certain dangers or exactly what to do, keep an extra eye out anyway. Regarding car safety, the AAP cautions:

- Do not allow your child to play or ride a tricycle in the street. Your child should play in a fenced yard or playground. Driveways are also dangerous.

- Walk behind your car before you back out of your driveway to be sure your child is not behind your car. You may not see your child through the rearview mirror.

Hide the Symbol

Index cards make great hide-and-seek items. They are also flexible in that you can write on them whatever you wish. For this activity, the suggested number for each round of play is five cards.

Materials
4" x 6" index cards
Crayon or marker

How to Do It

1. Write a symbol on each card. For numbers, make the range from one to five. For letters, go from A to E. For shapes, use a circle, square, triangle, rectangle, and oval. Other symbols are possible as well. Here are some suggestions: ?, !, @, (happy face), and (heart).

2. Hide the five related cards throughout another room.

3. Let a part of each card show so that your child can easily find each one.

4. Every time your child returns a card, say "You found the _____."

5. After a few repetitions of this game, your child is likely to say "the _____."

6. Let your child's recognition of the symbols happen naturally.

Behind the Scenes

Repetition and familiarity are the two main teaching tools here. That is why this kind of play is by group, with only five in each group. Because naming the symbol is not necessary, only a perk, the learning by these two processes is likely to come naturally. Another benefit of this game is visual discrimination expertise, the ability to recognize the uniqueness of each separate symbol. It is this skill that is fundamental for being ready for reading on the kindergarten level.

Research Roundup!

Having a strong vocabulary is important for success in school, according to "New Research: Two-Year-Old Vocabulary Predicts Kindergarten Success" by Aaron Loewenberg, MEd. Loewenberg, who taught kindergarten for four years, knows the importance of entering kindergarten with some basic literacy and math skills. He cites a study published in *Child Development* that shows "the seeds for kindergarten success and adulthood are planted years before children get to kindergarten," and found that children with larger vocabularies at age two entered kindergarten well-prepared both academically and behaviorally. He adds, "Students who enter kindergarten with advanced academic and behavioral skills typically experience greater opportunities as they grow older."

Go-Togethers

Many things in our world go together. You are likely to find such pairs right in your home.

Materials

Pairs of items that are safe for your child to handle

Behind the Scenes

Matching games are great fun now, and this version takes the concept up a notch. It requires understanding, and that kind of exercise will stand your child in good stead as logical reasoning continues to grow and develop.

Research Roundup!

The website of the American Academy of Pediatrics has intellectual insight related to your two-year-old. Leaving the more concrete level of thinking, your child is now becoming more thoughtful. He understands more language and is beginning to form mental images. Your two-year-old will be able to do much more in his head rather than actually having to manipulate objects. With memory and logical abilities expanding, you will see your little one understanding how things are related either exactly by shape or color or in a more abstract way, such as in a puzzle. Purpose will soon become evident. Your little one is learning about cause and effect, which may become obvious as he wants to wind toys, turn on and off lights, and even operate some appliances. You will also notice your child's play growing more complex. Instead of random activities, you are likely to see a favorite doll put to bed and even under a cover.

How to Do It

1. Collect several pairs of items that go together and put them on a table. Suggestions:

   - Shoe and sock
   - Pencil and paper
   - Bottle of water and cup
   - Knife and fork
   - Shirt and tie

2. Ask your child to pick out items that go together.

3. Take your turn.

4. If your child has difficulty, give as many hints as you wish.

All Sorts of Things

Use your ingenuity to find items around your house for sorting.

Materials

Items for sorting: blocks, colored paper clips, colored rubber bands, silverware, pencils, pens, socks, towels, toy cars, toy trucks, dolls

Behind the Scenes

While it is easy to think that the only way to carry out a sorting activity is by buying a toy-sorting game, now you have a whole different perspective. A quick look around the house could open up a whole new world.

Research Roundup!

"Child Development Tracker: Your Two-Year-Old" on PBS.org says that although every child's development is individual and complex, children still develop in a generally predictable sequence. Each child has his own stamp and pace and is also influenced by both environment and personal experiences. Two-year-olds play and complete their daily routines. They also learn important math skills. Just as they can use a toy to represent another object, they can recognize patterns and understand concepts of time such as *tomorrow* and *yesterday.* Two-year-olds also begin to use logical reasoning to solve everyday problems. They can sort items, complete puzzles with eight pieces or fewer, and stack a set of rings on a peg by size. They also understand addition and subtraction with the numbers one and two.

How to Do It

1. Take out your selection of items.

2. Be sure that you watch your child especially carefully if you select small items such as paper clips.

3. Determine the sorting specifications. For example, if you choose a set of blocks and three different colors, start the process by placing one of the blocks in the correct color grouping.

4. Take turns picking a block from the large group and placing it appropriately. There are many different items and many ways to group them. Color, size, and shape are the most common. However, you might think of other categories such as dolls with blonde, short, or curly hair and hair ties that have different textures.

Scribbling

This is a natural pastime. Use thick, washable markers or thick crayons for the best results.

Materials

Washable markers or thick crayons
2 9" x 12" sheets of paper or copy paper

Behind the Scenes

While no particular letters or recognizable shapes are expected, you have the opportunity in this free-form activity to lay the groundwork for what is to come. Just mentioning letter names and pointing out shapes provides background for writing development.

Research Roundup!

Michelle Anthony, PhD, explains the beginnings of literacy in "Early Literacy: Writing with 0–2 Year Olds." Because much of early writing literacy is the development of fine-motor abilities in the fingers and hands, playing while exercising these fine-motor skills is useful. Young children can grow these abilities, she says, by "using tools like washable chunky crayons, markers, scissors, tweezers, tongs, chalk, paintbrushes, etc." Even tearing paper will strengthen small muscles. Young children should play with blocks and things they can manipulate with their hands, such as playdough and finger-paint. Writing skills are also taught by modeling; show your two-year-old your writing when you are making your shopping list or signing birthday cards.

Gross-Motor and Fine-Motor Skills Progress

Pail Ball

Plastic beach pails are excellent for this activity. You also could use two small, clean, plastic wash basins.

How to Do It

1. Fill up a pail with a bunch of your child's folded socks. Anywhere from five to eight is a good number.

2. Give one pail to your child. Hold another one for yourself.

3. Show him how to throw all of his sock balls into your pail.

4. Move yours around to try to catch the socks as your little one throws them.

5. After you have all the socks in yours, throw them back to your child's pail. Encourage him to move his pail around so that he will always be in the best catching position.

6. If such a strategy seems too hard, you both can play while having your pails on the floor.

Materials

2 beach pails or wash basins
5-8 folded socks

Behind the Scenes

Throwing is part of your child's play, and this setup supports that skill constructively. You will find that the little sock balls are just the right size for your little one.

Research Roundup!

Beginning at about eighteen months old, you will begin to see your toddler get the hang of using his whole arm to throw a ball, according to "Throwing and Catching: Toddler Development" on babycentre.co.uk. Catching is more difficult and probably will not show up until about age three. For throwing indoors, use soft spongy balls or beanbags. Around this age, your child may enjoy the challenge of throwing a ball into a basket.

Play Ball

While most of the toys you need for your child are found around your house, there are a few simple basics worth acquiring. One is a ball made out of a soft material and about 7" to 10" in diameter. In addition, you might want to add beach balls of any size.

Materials

Beach ball or other soft ball

Behind the Scenes

The ball in this game makes a wonderful focus, and songs and rhymes can enrich the experience. They can be stimuli to new and creative ways to expand the play.

Research Roundup!

According to *Your Baby & Child: From Birth to Age Five* by Penelope Leach, the new aspect to play at this age is thinking. While rolling, catching, or kicking a ball was the focus before, now your two-year-old will take play further and imagine and create with it. With manual dexterity also improving at this time, ball play offers lots of options. If the play is quiet and predictable between the two of you, conversation might be beneficial. "By listening to her and thinking about her questions, you can keep abreast of her thought processes," Leach says. By talking together, you can exchange thoughts and insights and have a wonderful opportunity to give interesting information and novel ideas.

How to Do It

1. Sit opposite your child a few feet apart and roll away.

2. Move in closer or further apart, however you are most comfortable.

3. Stand up if you want to encourage throwing the ball to each other.

4. Roll or throw and make up your own games as you go.

5. Add singing or saying rhymes if you would like to enhance the fun of your play.

The Wheels on the Bus

This is one of the most popular songs for young children. It has several positive aspects. First of all, the tune is catchy and easy to learn. The words are logical and teach concepts, and the movements that go with the song promote coordination. Last, it lends itself to creativity—acting out the movements and being able to make up new ones.

How to Do It

1. Place the chairs in a row, one behind the other, and call it a bus.

2. Take your seats on the first two chairs. You be the driver the first time around and let your child take the driver's seat for the second.

3. Keep singing and rotating seats for as long as you continue to play.

4. Here are the basic words to the song. However, remember you can make up your own with your own creative actions:

   The Wheels on the Bus
   The wheels on the bus go 'round and 'round, 'round and 'round, 'round and 'round.
   The wheels on the bus go 'round and 'round, all through the town.
   The doors on the bus go open and shut, open and shut, open and shut.
   The doors on the bus go open and shut, all through the town.
   The wipers on the bus go swish, swish, swish, swish, swish, swish, swish, swish, swish.
   The wipers on the bus go swish, swish, swish, all through the town.
   The money on the bus goes clink, clink, clink, clink, clink, clink, clink, clink, clink.
   The money on the bus goes clink, clink, clink, all through the town.

Materials

4 or more chairs

Behind the Scenes

Like so many early childhood songs, the words to this song are beneficial to learning about the world. In addition, the physical actions given for the words provide opportunities for natural movement. Taken together, these two perspectives make up a solid play-and-learn happy song.

Research Roundup!

Singing to your child is calming and beneficial. Graham Welch, PhD, from the Institute of Education at the University of London reported those benefits from his study "The Physical, Psychological,

Social, Musical, and Educational Benefits of Singing." Welch finds that singing is "one of the most positive forms of human activity" there is.

Let's Run

Running is great exercise. This is a good time to teach it to your two-year-old as an "under-control" activity.

Materials

None

Behind the Scenes

Controlled exercise is a wonderful concept to begin at this time. Moving and moving fast are good for your two-year-old. However, most important for both of you is that your activities don't get out of hand. For your child's own security, he needs to always feel that you are in charge — and you need to feel that way too!

Research Roundup!

"Fitness and Your 2- to 3-Year-Old" on the early childhood education website kidshealth.org gives a full picture of two-year-olds on the move. "Kids this age are walking and running, kicking, and throwing." Some may be jumping too. Keep these skills in mind when encouraging your child to be active. Such opportunities are exactly what your little one needs to continue to improve and refine his motor skills. When you play active games together and provide age-appropriate active toys such as balls, push and pull toys, and riding vehicles, you will also be naturally successful. Mommy and Me programs can introduce tumbling, dance, and general movement. However, you don't have to enroll children in a formal program to foster these skills. Here are some excellent guidelines for at-home and outside play:

- At least thirty minutes of structured (adult-led) physical activity

- At least sixty minutes of unstructured (free play) physical activity

- Avoid more than one hour of inactivity at a time, except when sleeping

How to Do It

1. Go outside.

2. Pick a starting place.

3. Choose a short destination. Run to it together.

4. Have your child walk back to your starting line.

5. When you are both ready, give him the "ready, set, go" signal and have him run to you again.

6. Have your child go back to your starting line again and, when you are both ready, give him the "ready, set, go" signal for him to run to you.

7. Repeat this process for as long as you both enjoy it. Each time your child is ready to start again, ask him to run the distance a little faster.

8. A variation is that you can both go back to the starting line and run together to your destination.

Finger Exercises

Exercise is good for every part of your body, even your fingers. So it is for your child.

Materials

None

Behind the Scenes

This activity is derived from the practice of reflexology. Sometimes a little activity can make the biggest difference.

Research Roundup!

While similar to yoga for relaxing the body, reflexology is a practice specifically directed to the hands and the feet. Authors Mildred Carter and Tammy Weber discuss how reflexology can be beneficial for children in *Body Reflexology: Healing at Your Fingertips*. Children are the easiest subjects on whom to use reflexology because they are still attuned to nature. What is especially appropriate for children is the gentleness of the practice. By providing gentle rubs to special places on either hands or feet, such as the thumb, there is natural relief to other parts of the body.

How to Do It

1. Teach your child how to do these finger exercises.

2. Start by demonstrating on your child's fingers. Then do the exercises together.

3. Here are the instructions for each finger:

   - Wiggle it.
   - Massage it.
   - Stretch it.

Social Development with People, Places, and Things

My Story

All stories are interesting, but one about your child will be the most interesting of all.

Materials

4" x 6" photo album
4" x 6" index cards
Marker or crayon

Behind the Scenes

Including pictures of family members and friends in a personalized book helps to increase your two-year-old's awareness of special people. The reading enrichment is an added benefit of this social activity. More abstract thinking is on the way, and now you have this very specific book to foster the progress.

1. In the photo album, place photos that have your child and family and friends in them doing interesting things on the right.

2. On the left sides of the pages, place index cards and write three- or four-word sentences about the corresponding pictures on the other sides.

   I have new shoes.
   I like Grandma's house.
   Here is Emma!
   Uncle Anthony is fun.

3. As you read the story, point to the words as you say them and then point to the pictures. Feel free to have conversations about each sentence and the pictures.

Research Roundup!

Falling behind at play can turn into falling behind socially, according to a study by the Stavanger Project at the Norwegian Reading Centre, University of Stavanger in Norway. Project findings reported on ScienceDaily.com found that "while 70 percent of two-year-olds with normal language development function well when playing with other children, only 11 percent of two-year-olds with poor language skills play well with others." Children with poor language skills have problems keeping up when playing, and this causes other children to stop including them. Exclusion causes later long-term social effects.

Play Places

Because your two-year-old has a relatively short attention span, he is likely to enjoy changing activities quite frequently. A nice way to do that is by setting up different play places that include a variety of play items.

Materials

4 small blankets or sheets
Assorted toys

How to Do It

1. Spread each blanket or sheet in a different corner of the room in which you are playing.

2. Put different types of toys on each of the blankets or sheets. Here are some suggestions:

   - Puzzles
   - Paper with thick crayons
   - Blocks
   - Board books

3. Play classical music to start and then get settled to play together in one area.

4. Stop the music after ten to fifteen minutes and ask your child to choose another play area.

5. When you see that he is ready to play again, begin the music.

6. Repeat this process until you and your two-year-old have had the opportunity to play in each of the four areas.

Behind the Scenes

One of the big play problems at this stage is attention span. By setting up boundaries related to time and space, you address those difficulties head on and are likely to end up with extended, meaningful, and joyful play.

Research Roundup!

"Parents can increase the attention span of their child as early as during infancy by displaying interest in the same toy their child is playing with. Findings suggest that when a parent focused on a toy, the child paid attention to the same toy for a longer period of time, even continuing after the parent had looked away," according to Cari Neirenberg in the article "Simple Trick May Improve an Infant's Attention Span" on LiveScience.com.

Bouncing

This is a great opportunity to play in a loving free-form manner with this parent-child interaction, which comes naturally. There are many nursery rhymes and simple childhood songs that lead right into this kind of rhythmic activity.

Materials
None

Behind the Scenes
Bouncing is one of those activities that is known to be especially bonding for parents and their two-year-olds. Besides feeling good to little ones, it has an inherent parent attraction too.

Research Roundup!
In my book *Parent Involvement Begins at Birth*, I describe how important a loving parent-child relationship is right from the start and explain the lasting impact it has on future development. "Relationships are what social development is all about," and the parent-child one is the first and most important. All parent-child activities make a difference, and the key is that they offer "love, security, and respect to the child. Young children need to feel protected and cared for to be able eventually to care for themselves and others."

How to Do It

1. Sit on a bed, in your favorite chair, or on a couch with your child on your lap.

2. Bounce him up and down as long as he continues to enjoy the activity.

3. Say, "I love you," and any other nurturing words you wish.

4. Be sure you look at your child, smile, and laugh together.

5. If a particular children's song comes to mind, go ahead and sing it too.

Where Is It?

While family has an important nurturing influence on a developing young child, home plays a role as well. Your child will enjoy getting to know his home and many of the items in it.

Materials
Objects around the home

Behind the Scenes
New child understanding brings joy to a parent. While before your little one could follow simple directions, now he can handle a little more complexity. Your child will see your excitement, and you in turn are likely to notice how valued your special kind of appreciation is to your child.

Research Roundup!
In my book *Constructive Parenting*, there is an explanation about relationship development. After the first and most important parent-child relationship comes grandparents, siblings, aunts, uncles, cousins, and then close friends of the family. "The family is actually the training ground for all future

relationships, and the bulk of this exposure takes place in the first five years." All of these relationships continue to flourish in one way or another throughout a child's lifetime. Parents begin theirs with their child at birth. While that starts out as interactions in which they have total control over their baby, it turns into a process of relinquishing control to their child little by little over time. Day by day their baby, toddler, two-year-old, preschooler, school-age child, teenager, and then young adult learns more and more about the world around him.

How to Do It

1. Think of an object in another room and describe it.

2. Ask, "Where is the . . . ?"

3. Ask your child to please bring it to you.

4. If he brings the correct one, say, "Thank you very much."

5. If he does not, start the process again.

6. As soon as you receive five items, reverse the process. Point to one item and say "Where does the . . . belong?"

7. After your child tells you, or after you tell him if need be, ask him to please put the item back where it came from originally.

8. Continue until all items have been returned to their original places.

Dress-Up

Dressing up in parents' clothes has a great appeal for young children. It also provides practice for daily dressing skills.

Materials
Old clothes and accessories

Behind the Scenes
Open-ended play, with no beginning or end, is at the heart of this activity. While *open* is the major defining characteristic of this activity, boundaries are still needed. That is why a basket that you fill yourself and a designation of where to play are both included as part of the structure of this activity.

Research Roundup!
Open-ended play, as explained on the Play and Playground Encyclopedia website, allows children to express themselves freely and creatively without being bound by limitations. For traditional play

How to Do It

1. Set out a laundry basket with clothes.

2. Put in as many accessories as you have as well, such as ties, wallets, pocketbooks, jewelry, and scarves.

3. Let your child pretend and play freely with these.

Fun Baby Learning Games

materials, commonly chosen items are clay, sand, paint, blocks, and other materials that are free-form. There are no rules, expectations, or specific problems to solve, and there is no finished product as a goal. When playing with household materials, cardboard boxes and clothes that encourage dramatic play are commonly used. Pretend forts, tents, cars, and costumes all foster the imagination. For these, "a stick can become a knight's sword, a rock star's guitar, a cowboy's horse, a boat on a stream, or a slingshot with a rubber band." Specifically for two- and three-year-olds, realistic props such as dolls and play kitchens are appropriate. "All children love age-appropriate art supplies, such as paper, crayons, markers, paints, and scissors, which allow for hours of creative open-ended play."

Language Becomes Basic Conversation

Hand in Hand

Taking a walk provides an excellent venue for parent-child conversation. The more of these you two take, the more enriching this activity will become.

How to Do It

1. Take a walk with your child.
2. Let the conversation flow.

Materials
None

Behind the Scenes
This is definitely one of those gross-motor activities that has benefits far beyond a simple walk or run. Cognitive, social-emotional, language, and self-esteem development are all areas that can grow as part of this process.

Research Roundup!
The Dr. Sears website discusses best practices for talking to your two-year-old. His article "25 Ways to Talk So Children Will Listen" includes recommendations that should be helpful with your two-year-old.

1. Connect before you direct. Get down to your child's eye level and engage in eye-to-eye contact to get his attention.
2. Address the child. Always open your conversation with your child's name.
3. Stay brief. Use the one-sentence rule. It is important to be brief to give the idea that you know exactly what you mean.
4. Stay simple. Use as many short sentences with one-syllable words as you can. The younger the child, the shorter and simpler your sentences should be.
5. Be positive. Instead of "No running," try something like "Walk when inside."
6. Use etiquette when speaking with your child. Use *please* and *thank you* when talking with your two-year-old.

I Want

Being able to express yourself is important for success in life. "I want" can be used as a catalyst for proper sentence development.

Materials
None

Behind the Scenes
Because new language will continue to appear, it is helpful to keep providing guidance and support for your child's learning. "I want" will probably be a popular phrase with your two-year-old, so this little activity can foster using it in a pleasant and fun way.

Research Roundup!
According to the American Academy of Pediatrics, two-year-olds not only understand most of what you say, but they also speak with a rapidly growing vocabulary of about fifty words or more. What is on the horizon now is two- or three-word sentences such as "Drink juice" and "Mommy want cookie." Following that will be four-, five-, or even six-word sentences, such as, "Where's the ball, Daddy?" and "Dolly, sit in my lap." Two-year-olds also begin to use pronouns such as *I*, *you*, *me*, *we*, and *they*. This is followed by the concept of *mine* with examples, such as "I want my cup" and "I see my mommy." The AAP points out, "As a general rule, boys start talking later than girls, but this variation tends to even out as children reach school age."

How to Do It

1. Take turns starting a sentence with "I want."

2. Try to fulfill each other's wish. Here are some examples:

   - "I want the book." The other person brings the book.

   - "I want the green pillow." The other person brings the green pillow.

   - "I want the magazine." The other person brings the magazine.

Big and Small

You and your child have many of the same things. The difference is that yours are big, and his are small. While you are focusing on teaching your child the concepts of *big* and *small*, he will also have the opportunity to build his vocabulary with many new clothing words.

Materials
Clothing items: shirt, pants, socks, shoes, belt, hat, etc.

Behind the Scenes
Playing is at the heart of this "big and small" activity. Earlier in the book I described some advice important for the first year and for many years to come:

1. Play — Have fun!

2. Act natural — Be yourself.

3. Respond — Pay attention.

4. Touch — Hug and hold.

Use these principles and enjoy this activity as you play with your child in a fun and productive way.

Research Roundup!

In "Academic Learning in 0–2 Year Olds" by Michelle Anthony, PhD, on scholastic.com, the concept of size is right on target for teaching to your two-year-old. Other related concepts that could fit well with attention to size are shapes, colors, and the recognition of simple pictures of objects. Working with your child to group or separate objects along one of the above-mentioned dimensions" is developmentally appropriate at this time. Giving your child real objects to order or match according to your chosen parameter is an excellent way to design all different kinds of activities just for fun. According to the article, there are concepts that are likely to be mastered before age three.

- Understanding *larger*, *smaller*, and *longer*

- Pointing to body parts when asked

- Repeating two to three numbers in a row

- Responding to a request to put something in or take it out

- Being aware of opposites such as *wet* and *dry* and *soft* and *hard*

- Reacting to cause and effect appropriately; expecting that if something drops, someone will pick it up

Patterns

Colored paper is easily available and can be used in many ways. For this activity, select three sheets in different colors. Red, yellow, and blue or green are recommended colors, but any three will work.

Materials

3 sheets of different-colored paper
Scissors (adult use)

How to Do It

1. Go into your child's room and set out five items of clothing.

2. After all your child's items are laid out, bring a match from your own clothing for each item.

3. Take turns finding the items you each name. You can call out to each other phrases such as:

- Big hat
- Small shoes
- Big belt

Behind the Scenes

This pattern activity should be easy and fun for both of you. While your child can grow with whatever you create while teaching patterns, conversational language will grow by leaps and bounds within your play.

Research Roundup!

In a Q&A from the Mayo Clinic website, Jay L. Hoecker, MD, says, "Although every child grows and develops at his or her own pace, toddler speech development tends to follow a fairly predictable path." Here are brief guidelines for the average two-year-old:

- Speaks at least 50 words

- Links two words together, such as "my cup" or "no juice"

- Speaks clearly enough for parents to understand about half of the words

How to Do It

1. Cut each sheet in quarters.

2. Set up a pattern with three different colors.

3. Have your child match your pattern.

4. Have him make a pattern with three different colors for you to match.

5. Help your child as much as needed.

6. Continue play like this for as long as you two continue to enjoy it. After a while, you may want to make longer patterns.

Reading Time VI

You can make reading on this level participatory. Keep communication in mind. The idea behind all reading activities is to communicate a message to your child.

Materials

Children's book with rhyming words

Behind the Scenes

Books with rhyming words in them are best for this fill-in-the-last-word activity because the rhyming sounds are easiest to remember. However, if you select a book without rhyming words that your child really likes and has heard you read many times, it can still work well for this activity. The participatory part of this activity is what is most important.

Research Roundup!

Guidance from the Department of Education's website, "Start Early, Finish Strong: How to Help Every Child Become a Reader," discusses the tremendous potential of parents as aides for children who are learning to read. Recent research into human brain development is showing that parents

How to Do It

1. Choose your book to read together.

2. After you have read the story many times to your child, leave out the last word on each page and encourage your child to say it before you do.

truly are their children's first teachers and that what parents do, or do not do, has a lasting effect on their child's future reading skill and literacy. Reading regularly to a child has a direct positive relationship on that child's later reading achievement. Children develop much of their capacity for learning in the first three years of life, and this is the time when brains grow to 90 percent of their eventual adult size. As parents read, sing, and talk to their children, brain cells grow.

Self-Esteem Bursts with Growth over Attention to Self

Look at Me!

Any positive attention you give to your child will help make him feel important. There are no limits to what you can notice and reflect back to your two-year-old.

Materials
None

Behind the Scenes
Two-year-olds can be difficult because they often seek negative attention. With this kind of rhyming activity, you should see that need diminished. The more you give this kind of positive recognition to your little one, the less you should see some of those other troublesome and difficult reactive behaviors.

Research Roundup!
In my book *Constructive Parenting,* I say that building self-esteem requires a process of paying positive attention and talking to your child about his uniqueness. That means the parents' job is to "reflect on a daily basis his or her delight in the 'child's magnificent individuality.'" If you follow this pattern consistently over time, your child will develop self-confidence and self-esteem. While there is some kind of

How to Do It

1. Teach your child to say this fun rhyme, "Look at me. What do you see?"

2. Once you get a good start, give some possible responses, such as:

   - A happy face
   - A blue shirt
   - Brown hair

3. Teach your child to repeat the rhyme with the right timing, to get great responses.

4. Take your turn, too.

5. Point to different parts of your body and clothes, and encourage responses from your child.

natural pull to compare children to others, this strong commitment to keep looking for the good and reflecting it back to your child will help a lot. Here are some practical examples that you might want to use as is or modify.

- Your smile is irresistible.

- I see the twinkle in your eyes.

- You have soft cheeks.

- Look at your long wavy hair.

- You did that all by yourself.

Two Is Good

Age is an important concept that makes children proud, and adults too. Be sure that your child becomes well-versed in saying *two* for his age and showing two fingers.

Behind the Scenes

Showing two fingers and saying *two* is a way to exhibit self-pride. The combination of the words and the actions is what makes the effect so meaningful.

Research Roundup!

"An intuitive sense of number begins at a very early age. Children as young as two years of age can confidently identify one, two, or three objects before they can actually count with understanding" says Jenni Way in her article, "Number Sense Series: Developing Early Number Sense." The skill seems to be based on the mind's ability to form stable mental images of patterns and associate them with number. However, if the numbers are arranged in consistent patterns, the ability to recognize the groups becomes much easier, and the value of the number groups goes much higher. With two-year-old children, number activities are best done with moveable objects such as counters, blocks, and small toys.

How to Do It

1. Say this little rhyme with your child.

   Parent: How old are you?
   Child: I know I'm two.

2. Teach your child to say his part as loudly and clearly as possible.

3. Show him how to put up two fingers when saying *two*.

Computer Time

While your child probably has had some experience watching you in front of a computer, this is a wonderful time to teach him some beginning skills.

Materials
Computer

Behind the Scenes

While it is not recommended to foster screen time for little ones, providing exposure to your child under your direction is recommended. This activity follows the concept that this kind of guided computer time is a gesture of positive attention.

How to Do It

1. Sit with your child on your lap.

2. Open a child-appropriate website of your choice.

3. Explain to your child what you are doing and what you are seeing on the screen.

4. Let your child participate with you in whatever way seems appropriate for him.

How much screen time is okay for children? According to the American Academy of Pediatrics, "Some screen time is okay for children as young as eighteen months, but the organization recommends limiting kids to an hour or less a day of high-quality digital media—and urges parents to stay very much involved when their kids are using screens." Of course, these guidelines would never need to be set if little ones were not watching these devices, but they are. According to a Common Sense Media survey, "One in five parents say they know the AAP recommendations for their child's media use," while half are unaware of the recommendations.

Here We Go 'Round the Mulberry Bush

Circle games are fun and are ideal for engaging young children. The "This is the way we . . ." part of this play will allow your child to be as dramatic as he would like.

How to Do It

1. While moving in a clockwise direction, sing the words to this song with your child. Each time you sing a stanza, include an activity, such as "wash the clothes" or "cook the food." When the creative part comes, do some motions.

2. Encourage your child to do similar motions with you. Here are the words:

   Here we go round the mulberry bush, the mulberry bush, the mulberry bush.
   Here we go round the mulberry bush so early in the morning.
   This is the way we (wash the clothes, cook the food, iron the shirts . . .)
   This is the way we (wash the clothes, cook the food, iron the shirts . . .)
   So early in the morning.

3. Do one motion at a time and then return to the beginning of the song again.

4. Make up as many motions as you would like.

Behind the Scenes

This is one of those "I can do it" children's songs. The combination of action words with simple tasks work together to create an appropriate child-centered feeling of power and accomplishment.

Research Roundup!

"The Surprising Meaning and Benefits of Nursery Rhymes" by Michael Sizer on PBS.org dissects the meaning of rhymes and how and why they have survived. Because the origins date back so far, there is no real age specification for any of them. The differences are just in how we use them with children of different ages today. Nursery rhymes may be beneficial to four identified areas:

- **Brain development.** "Not only does the repetition of rhymes and stories teach children how language works, it also builds memory capabilities."

- **Culture.** They preserve a culture that spans generations and provide something in common for generations in a family, a shared ritual.

- **Confidence.** They allow young children, even shy ones, to feel confident singing, dancing, and performing.

Video Time

It is quite easy these days to record your two-year-old in action. Playing the recording makes the activity fun for you both.

Materials
None

Behind the Scenes
The more you focus attention on your child and what he can do, the better he will feel about himself. It is one thing for your child to succeed at his actions, but the experience is magnified when he can see it being played back on video.

How to Do It

1. Encourage your child to sing, dance, or perform any other activity of choice.

2. Record the part of it that you especially like and that you think will be most interesting and meaningful for your child to see.

Research Roundup!
PBS Parents' "Child Development Tracker: Your Two-Year-Old" provides a realistic way to interpret your child's current skills and abilities. "There is no one like your child. Every child's development is unique and complex." Although children develop through a generally accepted sequence of milestones, they may not proceed through these in the same way as others or at the same time. A child's development is also greatly influenced by his environment and his personal experiences. In general, two-year-old children enjoy using their senses and motor skills to explore. They also can usually solve simple problems with a trial-and-error method. Sometimes you will see your two-year-old practice an activity many times to master it. Children this age also pretend more as they play.

Fun Baby Learning Games

8 Thirty to Thirty-Six Months

Keeping a schedule is very important now and should be used to guide your two-and-a-half-year-old through each day. She has now developed, or is in the process of developing, many adult-like characteristics. She should be able to walk easily up and down stairs, speak in sentences, ask for what she wants, and ride a tricycle.

The idea now is to help your older two-year-old stick to routines as much as possible. Three balanced meals a day at regular times, an exercise/play routine, and ten to twelve hours of sleep are recommended. Enjoy the opportunity to help your child make this exciting transition.

Getting to Three

Relish watching your little one's awareness deepen. While you will continue to see vestiges of impatient and somewhat self-centered two-year-old behavior, you will also enjoy the pleasure of a growing child chiming in with good ideas and a helpful spirit.

Milestones of Development

- Better understands size
- Better understands spatial relations
- Expanded comprehension of numbers
- Knowledge of similarities
- Sorts items
- Better understanding of the part/whole relationship
- Manipulates playdough and clay
- Stacks about eight blocks
- Runs
- Improves walking balance
- Walks upstairs with alternating feet
- Coordinates a two-handed activity
- Takes pride in achievements, resists help
- Puts on clothes with supervision
- Identifies object by description of what it does
- Follows simple directions

Cognitive Growth and Concepts

Outside

Being outside is an experience all its own. Have fun with the stimulation it can bring to you and your child. Get ready for questions. Your child is likely to have many.

Materials
None

Behind the Scenes
Curiosity runs very high with your two-and-a-half-year-old. While answers to some of her questions will roll right off your tongue, other questions will stop you in your tracks. If you don't know the answer, tell her that you will find it together. You may want to visit your local library or bookstore to read more on topics that interest your child. The iternet is also an amazing resource to handle those hard-to-answer questions.

Research Roundup!
Effective communication comes about in exactly the same way that it does with adults, by talking about interests, says Lauren Lowry, author of "What Makes Your Child Tick? Using Children's Interests to Build Communication Skills." As with adults, Lowry finds "children are more likely to interact, pay attention, and learn new words" when the conversation is based on their interests. Parents could

How to Do It

1. Let your child be the leader of this activity. Go outside or look out a window, and ask her, "What do you see?" There are many possible answers, such as trees, a car, a house, and so on.

2. Follow up with a nice conversation about each of the items she has shown interest in. You are likely to hear many who, what, where, when, and why questions. Take the opportunity to give the best answers you can, or look up answers to questions that you two can research together.

identify a common child interest, such as cars or trucks. To engage your child's interest on this topic, try the following:

- While playing with cars, you can pretend to fill them up with gas.

- When you go through a car wash together, you can talk about what is happening.

- When you see a car moving rapidly, you can say, "Wow, that car is going fast!"

More or Less

Sometime around seven years old, your child will learn to *conserve* or get the idea that as you change volume from one shape to another, the amount of a substance will stay the same. Many parents like to play this game now to grow a child's understanding, well before this developmental skill is actually achieved.

Materials
Short, wide glass
Tall, thin glass

How to Do It

1. Fill the short glass with water.

2. Pour the water into the tall, thin one.

3. Have fun with these questions:

   - Is it more now?
   - Is it the same?

Behind the Scenes
The ability to evaluate the same amount in different-sized containers is called *conservation*. When posed with the above situation, your two-and-a-half-year-old will probably not be able to give you the right answer. Be advised that not being able to do so has nothing to do with intelligence. It simply shows that your child is on target and not quite ready to learn this higher-level cognitive skill. Even so, exposure to this process is stimulating for her mind.

Research Roundup!
This concept of conservation is thought to develop over time, from age two to seven. Even a child of three years typically shows no evidence yet of this kind of understanding. In *Early Education: Three, Four, and Five Year Olds Go to School,* by Carol Seefeldt and Barbara Wasik, this kind of play is discussed. "Eric is shown two cups; one cup is tall and thin and the second cup is short and wide. Both hold the same amount of juice. Eric's mom pours juice from the tall, thin cup into the short, wider cup, showing him that the same amount of juice fits into both glasses. When asked what glass of juice he wants, Eric replies, 'I want this,' pointing to the tall glass, 'because I am really thirsty and I want more juice; Eric chooses this glass due to its height." At this age, children are still concrete thinkers and solve problems like this based on physical features.

Stick to It

What two-year-old doesn't like stickers? Have fun with these sticker index cards by making matches and hiding them around the room.

How to Do It

1. Place a sticker on an index card, and let your child place a matching sticker on another index card.

2. Continue making index card pairs.

3. Once you have completed five sets of matching cards, you are ready for many variations of play. Here are several:

   - Set out a row of sticker cards and a pile of matching ones. Take turns picking from the pile and placing your card on its correct match.

   - Turn all the unmatched pairs face down. Play a matching game by trying to make as many matches as you can by flipping a card over and finding its mate. Use as many or as few cards as appropriate for your child.

   - Place one set of sticker cards in hiding places around the room. Give your child one card at a time to find its match.

4. Make up your own sticker-matching activities to play together.

Materials
Set of stickers
4" x 6" index cards

Behind the Scenes
Keep your first matching cards to distinct pictures. As your child gets more experienced, you can make them more difficult to distinguish.

Research Roundup!
How Kids Develop, a collaborative project of several San Diego organizations, provides an overview of different aspects of development in this exciting year from age two to three. Here are a few basics related to cognitive development:

- Understanding simple stories

- Pretending with dolls and stuffed animals

- Matching familiar items to pictures of those items

- Putting together three- to four-piece puzzles

- Beginning to "play" house

- Naming pictures of objects and pointing to pictures of people doing familiar activities

- Counting "one, two, three" and understanding what those numbers mean

Laundry Sorting

Having your child help you with tasks is often frustrating. However, laundry sorting and folding can work quite well as a little one's activity.

Materials
Fresh laundry

Behind the Scenes
Emphasis at this age should be on regular life activities and having your little one participate in them in meaningful ways. Making a contribution to getting a job done is directly related to building self-esteem. Matching socks into pairs and sorting exercise thinking skills, allowing your child to practice fine-motor skills at the same time. Talking to your child about when different garments are worn enriches cognitive development. To broaden your child's awareness even more, add specifics about how certain types of clothes are saved for special occasions.

Research Roundup!
The Center for Parenting Education states that children who do chores at home "have higher self-esteem, are more responsible, and are better able to deal with frustration and delayed gratification," qualities that are considered by educators to contribute to greater success in school. According to the center's website, researcher Marty Rossman finds that performing those tasks has lasting impact in that "the best predictor of young adults' success in their mid-twenties was that they participated in household tasks when they were three or four."

How to Do It

1. Show your child how to make separate piles of individual types of clothing.

2. Show her how to fold items such as underwear, washcloths, and socks.

3. Your two-and-a-half-year-old might even be able to help you fold larger items such as hand towels.

Paper Plate Play

Do you remember coloring on paper plates and how much fun it was when you pressed your crayon on the fluted edges? If you do, you probably would not want your child to miss that opportunity.

How to Do It

1. Take a paper plate and begin your creative coloring.

2. Here are some ideas to use when you are finished coloring:

   - Cut one of the colored plates in half. Then take turns matching it back together. After you have had fun with halves, move on to quarters. You might even want to try thirds. Be sure to use the terms *half*, *quarter*, and *thirds* when you play with your child.

   - Make some happy-face designs. You can even cut out two eyes, a nose, and a mouth and wear the plates as masks.

   - Write numbers from one to twelve around the paper plate to make a clock face.

   - Attach to the center of the plate, with a brass fastener, two hands made out of colored paper strips. Then have fun with your child introducing time on the hour. Do not expect your child to know this concept, but it's never too early to start talking about time.

Materials

Paper plates
Crayons
Children's scissors

Behind the Scenes

This activity aids in cognitive development in the following ways:

- Two-, three-, and four-piece puzzles teach the concepts of halves, quarters, and thirds

- Eyes, nose, and mouth placement on a face teaches vocabulary and body-part locations

- Exposes the child to numbers from one through twelve, along with telling time by the hour

There are also opportunities for growth in the other areas of development:

- Fine-motor coloring and cutting practice

- Social-emotional pretend play with masks

- Language enrichment through interactions

- Self-esteem development connected with creation and accomplishment

Research Roundup!

Researchers are learning more about how the creative process works in the brain. While it is an extremely complicated subject, in "Beautiful Minds: The Real Neuroscience of Creativity," writer Scott Barry Kaufman explains that "the right brain/left brain distinction does not offer us the full picture of how creativity is implemented." Instead, the creative process relies on "many interacting cognitive processes . . . and emotions."

Motor Skills Basics Keep Getting Better

Building

You will be able to enjoy two parts of this activity with your child, the free-form creative aspect and the fun of copying each other. This is one of the best activities for developing spatial relationships and eye-hand coordination. Free-form work is the beginning, and the copying part lays the groundwork for future map-reading skills.

Materials

Building materials: blocks, bottle caps, small flat wooden sticks, dominoes, etc.

Behind the Scenes

Projects and focused play are beginning, and those are giant steps in the realm of independent play. Open-ended activities let the child maintain direction, flow, and the ability to work toward specific goals.

> ## How to Do It
>
> 1. Select your building material.
> 2. Suggestions for carrying out the activity:
>   - Create freely with your child, side by side.
>   - Build with your child on the same building project.
>   - Make a small model for your child to copy. Watch your child design a simple structure, and then you copy that one.

Research Roundup!

Blocks rock, according to writer Gwen Dewar on ParentingScience.com. Blocks and other construction toys are credited with being able to change the way children think. Building projects are thought to stimulate creativity and sharpen crucial learning skills. Studies suggest that they boost ability in these areas:

- Motor and eye-hand coordination
- Spatial relationships
- Creative and divergent thinking
- Social-emotional development
- Language

Other benefits include pretend-play growth and links with later advanced math skills.

Balance Walking

Walking a straight path is fine for this activity. After your child gets comfortable with it, you might want to give a little curve to it.

Materials
Masking tape or painter's tape

Behind the Scenes
As you know from toddler time, a child is a little unsteady when first learning to walk. As your child grows, balance keeps improving, and walking keeps getting better. With no more than a few rough edges in the balance area now, your child is likely to find walking on this very safe and secure "balance beam" as one of her favorite kinds of play.

How to Do It

1. Make a masking-tape path wide enough for your child to walk on without falling off. Make it go across a room or down a hallway.

2. Take turns walking on the path.

3. If your child needs it, you can hold her hand when she is trying to stay on the line that you made.

Research Roundup!
All children are different and develop at different rates. While most every skill develops at its own pace, Amanda Morin writes on Understood.org that children over the age of two should be learning to do the following:

- Walk, run, and start to jump with both feet

- Pull or carry toys while walking

- Throw and kick a ball; try to catch with both hands

- Stand on tiptoes and balance on one foot

- Climb on furniture and playground equipment

- Walk upstairs, holding onto the railing; may alternate feet

Water Fun

You can do this activity during bath time. You can also set it up in a play pool, large basin, or sink.

Materials
Pouring equipment: measuring cups, ladle, funnel, plastic cups, plastic bottles

Behind the Scenes
Open-ended play should continue to be a part of your child's day. Water play fits right in and will be especially helpful at bath time or during any other water-play opportunities.

Research Roundup!

Professor Carol M. Gross writes in "Science Concepts Young Children Learn through Water Play" that water play functions as "a key science and mathematics medium that enhances young children's learning through discovery." Water and a variety of small plastic containers can provide a wonderful sensory and learning experience. Free play with water in many different venues can lay the foundation for many scientific concepts, such as:

- Physics (flow, motion)

- Chemistry (solutions, cohesion)

- Biology (plant and animal life)

- Mathematics (measurement, equivalence, volume)

Mastery of these concepts will support understanding of many academic subjects in later schooling and life. "Children inquire, observe, compare, imagine, invent, design experiments, and theorize when they explore natural science materials such as water, sand, and mud," says Gross.

Step Up and Step Down

Walking up stairs is a great exercise for any age. Your child will be fine with a few steps to go up. If you do not have a staircase available, you can use a stepstool for your child.

Materials
Stepstool (optional)

Behind the Scenes
This is another one of those perfect activities designed to promote one particular area—motor in this case—that also fosters growth in the other four. Look how this activity shapes up:

- **Motor:** the gross-motor skill of being able to go up and down stairs and also the opportunity for exercise

- **Cognitive:** teaching beginning counting with one-to-one correspondence related to the steps

- **Social-Emotional:** having an activity to do together

- **Language:** the opportunity to learn a fun rhyme

- **Self-Esteem:** climbing steps successfully

How to Do It

1. Fill up the bathtub (or other alternative) with water. **Safety note: Never leave your child unattended around water.**

2. Add a variety of pouring equipment.

3. Your child will take over from there.

How to Do It

1. Take your child's hand and walk up three steps.

2. Turn around and walk down three steps.

3. Here is a rhyme to go with your climb:

   One, two, three; look at me.
   Three, two, one; that was fun.

4. If you would like your child to climb higher, try this:

   Four, five six; lots of tricks.
   Six, five, four; now no more.

"Is Your Child Struggling to Walk Up or Down Stairs?" on childandfamilydevelopment.com explains that going upstairs for a toddler is much easier than going down. That is mentioned purely as a caution to make sure that when you are around stairs with your little one, you are always available to help with the return trip down. However, the primary focus of the article is to be on the lookout for any delay. Using the timeline below, if you suspect a problem, do not hesitate to contact a physical therapist to find out if any formal therapy is needed. Maybe just a little guidance can be enough.

- On average, by nine to twelve months, children can crawl up stairs.

- On average, two-year-old children can take steps two feet per step, while holding a rail or one hand.

- By two-and-a-half, children can typically walk upstairs independently, two feet per step, without any support.

- Around age three, children can walk up- and down-stairs, one foot per step, while holding a rail.

- On average, by age three, children can walk up- and down-stairs, one foot per step, with no support.

"As a general rule, most children should be able to walk up and down stairs independently and alternating feet by the end of their third year."

Playdough

This play started with mud pies and now happens with playdough and other similar variations. Such play is nature's way of helping your child develop her small-muscle strength.

Materials
Playdough or similar material

Behind the Scenes
Playdough and its many available substitutes are designed to be convenient, safe substances for your little one to practice fine-motor skills and be creative at the same time. There are many plastic tools available for this kind of play, but they are not necessary. The substance itself, with all your child's pretend-play skills, is all you really need to enjoy this kind of playtime fun.

How to Do It

1. Sit opposite your child with each of you having your own ball of playdough or a similar material.

2. Be as creative as you and your child wish with the following steps:

3. Roll the playdough or other material into a ball with the palm of the hand.

4. Pat the ball flat into a pancake with the palm of the hand.

5. Make a happy face in the pancake with the index finger.

6. Roll the pancake into a long snake roll with both palms and fingers.

7. Set aside a small piece of the long snake roll. Coil the rest of the long snake roll into the shape of a bowl. Use the small piece to make objects to go into the bowl.

Research Roundup!

"Playdough Power" from NAEYC for Families discusses the benefits young children receive through this play. "This simple preschool staple lets children use their imaginations and strengthen the small muscles in their fingers" at the same time. Because of how appealing it is, playdough also serves to promote social skills such as sharing, taking turns, and enjoying being with other people. Because this play has no rules, it is considered open-ended play, a style that lets children feel competent. There is language growth through talking; science learning through hands-on experiences; math expertise by measuring and counting; and physical development through poking, rolling, and squishing. According to recent research, using your fingers and hands actually stimulates your brain and increases the number of neural connections it makes.

Social Time and Your Little One

My Family

Family is the training ground for all future relationships. The variety of ages, personalities, and genders of family members and close friends of the family affect your child's unique growth and development. Interactions with these people will make your child feel valued, needed, important, and proud of herself. While family members and close friends of the family are often far away, photographs can help keep them in your child's life by bringing back some memories of time spent together.

Materials

4" x 6" photo album
Family photos
Glue stick or tape

Behind the Scenes

With photo books, you have the opportunity to look at them over and over and continue to talk about the people in them at any time.

Research Roundup!

In my book *Parent Involvement Begins at Birth*, I discuss how vital parent involvement is to children's development, as "time spent with children ages birth to three defines their world." Through familiar regular routines, children learn values, self-discipline, work and play habits, and other important personal development characteristics. "Simple daily habits provide a secure and stable environment for children." While all can be orchestrated by an alternative caregiver such as a babysitter or other designated person, it is best done by a parent or grandparent, aunt, uncle, cousin, or close friend of the family. The critical link is love. In my book I quote Urie Bronfenbrenner, former longtime professor at Cornell University and one of the founding members of Head Start, who said that a child "needs the enduring, irrational involvement of one or more adults." When asked what was meant by "irrational involvement," he said, "Somebody has to be crazy about the kid."

How to Do It

1. On all the right-hand pages of the photo album, put in photos of family and some very close friends.

2. On the left-hand pages, print the names that go with the photos.

3. Read the book to your child by first pointing to the name on the left and then saying it.

4. Point to the corresponding photo on the right-hand page and say the same name. Continue in this way throughout the book.

What's Happening?

Children's magazines are your best bet for finding child-oriented pictures. However, catalogs and some mailings could be great sources.

Materials

Children's magazines
Construction paper
Glue stick or tape

Behind the Scenes

Spending time with your child is key. According to the U.S. Department of Education, "spending time with children and doing things together are the twin pillars of school readiness."

How to Do It

1. Select about five to ten pictures that portray interesting but fun-looking situations. Cut them out and paste each one on colored construction paper.

2. Place all of the pictures in a pile, facedown.

3. Take turns picking a picture and talking about it. Always start your play with "What's happening?" If your child does not have too much to say, ask some open-ended questions such as:

   - Who is in the picture?
   - Where are the people?
   - When is this scene taking place?
   - Why is he so happy, sad, angry, etc.?
   - How did he get there?

Research Roundup!

In *Your Baby & Child: From Birth to Age Five* by Penelope Leach, there is guidance about adult-child conversations. "The more you talk to your child, the better." However, there are real specifications related to your talking and how effective it will be. First and foremost, what you say needs to be interesting to your child, or it will have no value at all. Another qualification is that it must be in sync in some way with her own ideas and also must be positive. If parent-child talk is to be useful, it must have genuine give-and-take and not just be talk. If you start to use "uh-huh" and "Really?" what you are saying will be no more effective than the background noise of a radio, and your child will stop participating. Monologues from adults are hurtful to children as well. Pauses for child contributions are very important and a must for a meaningful two-way conversation.

Resting

In today's busy world, you will often find that your child's schedule is quite programmed. Whether your two-year-old goes to a preschool program, has child care at home, or just participates in many different activities, there will always be a need for movement from place to place and the need to hurry. Given this common hectic lifestyle, true rest is a concept to be fostered and valued. Soothing music will help put you both in the mood for relaxation.

Materials

Classical or other soothing music

Behind the Scenes

You both are likely to love this very special part of your day. You can even set it up with a timer so that you make sure that you do not shortchange yourselves on this valuable allotted time. The only requirement is to stay in your selected places, listen to the music, and more or less do nothing in particular.

Research Roundup!

Music has a powerful, positive effect on brain development, according to Susan Hallam, Institute of Education, University of London. An article in *Parents* magazine by Lori Kase Miller follows this thought, as she finds that as babies babble to learn language, "they also babble musically." Daniel Levitin, PhD, author of *This Is Your Brain on Music*, says that babies can make up songs, and with that, "create various musical ideas" of their own.

> ## How to Do It
>
> 1. Turn on some classical music or some other soothing music you like.
>
> 2. Find a sofa or comfortable chair, put your feet up, and relax. Encourage your child to find her own special spot as well.
>
> 3. Relax and enjoy your chosen music as long as your child enjoys listening.

How Does It Work?

You will see your child push, pull, turn, and open and shut everything in sight. Now is the time to channel that interest.

Materials

Toys to manipulate: toy car, pull toy, small plastic jar with a lid, small box with a cover, three-minute timer, and so on

Behind the Scenes

Fostering fine-motor skills in a fun way is excellent for your child's development. Keeping the activity focused by the boundaries of one special box enhances the effectiveness of this kind of play.

> ## How to Do It
>
> 1. Provide your child with a special box of toys.
>
> 2. Put inside this box whatever you can find that is safe and appropriate for your child that will push, pull, turn, and open and shut.
>
> 3. Enjoy engaging with your child as she plays with the assorted toys.

Research Roundup!

Fine-motor development, which refers to movements with the small muscles of the hands, starts in a very primitive way when babies start to use their hands to explore their own bodies and the world around them, according to Children's Therapy and Family Resource Centre. However, it is not until after their whole body starts to become more stable that fine motor as a true skill starts to progress. Cognitive and social-emotional development are two other areas that need to reach a certain level of sophistication before specific levels of eye-hand coordination can take place. *Push, pull, turn, open,* and *shut* are all examples of movements that rely on a basic amount of full-body development combined with an adequate level of cognitive and social-emotional functioning to be possible.

Outfit Matching

Your child is learning about dressing herself, and outfit matching can be an enjoyable activity to help her learn about the process.

Materials

5 shirts
5 pairs of shorts or pants

Behind the Scenes

This activity fosters the basic skills of learning to dress. There is no need now for your child to make the same pairs that you would make; the important part of this process is that your child is taking part and giving her input.

Research Roundup!

Getting dressed seems simple but requires multiple skills, including "bilateral coordination, right/left discrimination, postural stability, and motor planning," according to an article by Lauren Weichman titled "Dressing Skills: Developmental Steps for Kids." As a parent, it can be difficult to know at what age a child has these skills and to what degree, so these guidelines demonstrate what is considered doable and enjoyable for age two-and-a-half:

- Removes pull-down elastic-waist pants

- Unbuttons large buttons

- Puts on front-button shirt

3. As a child nears three years of age, she should be able to:
    - Put on socks and shoes, though they might be on the wrong feet or the socks might be inside-out

    - Put on pullover shirts with some help

    - Button large buttons

    - Pull down pants

    - Zip and unzip, with help to place on track

How to Do It

1. Set out the clothing.

2. Have your child put pairs together one by one. In this setting, there are no wrong choices, but you can still give your opinion and explain why.

Language Is Prevalent and Becoming Refined

Puppet Talk

Puppets are a great stimulus to conversing with your child. Homemade or store-bought puppets are fine to use with this activity. You can make your own puppets using old socks.

Materials
Puppets or stuffed animals

Behind the Scenes
Conversation is beneficial in many ways. Because correcting speech could put a damper on your play, the best thing to do when you hear an error is to repeat the word, phrase, or sentence correctly.

Research Roundup!
Children love puppets for different reasons at different stages of development, according to Jill Stamm, PhD, author of *Boosting Brain Power.* She recommends using colorful puppets as a language starter to help children begin conversations. As a toddler gets older, she may emotionally connect with the puppet and feel comfortable taking more control with it.

How to Do It
1. Select a puppet or stuffed animal for yourself and your child.
2. Start the conversation with your puppet or stuffed animal.
3. Encourage your child to speak back through hers.

Penny Fun

This remembering skill grows over time, so try playing this activity often to hone your toddler's skills.

Materials
10 pennies

Behind the Scenes
This is a simple, fun game to do with your child beginning now and from time to time. The years between two and seven are called preoperational. This is a time that conservation skills begin to develop, but these skills are usually not honed until much closer to the seven-year-old mark. The term, *conservation*, as defined on SimplyPsychology.org, means "the understanding that something stays the same in quantity even though its appearance changes . . . conservation is the ability to understand that redistributing material does not affect its mass, number, volume, or length."

How to Do It
1. Place ten pennies in a row.
2. Count them with your child.
3. Place all the pennies closer together.
4. Ask your child if these are fewer or the same as you had before. "The same" is the right answer, but if your child says "fewer," explain that the pennies are still the same, just closer together.

Research Roundup!

Psychologist Jean Piaget originally identified the idea of the concrete operational stage in the 1960s based on development he observed with his own children. He categorized stages of development and found this particular level of understanding rare before the age of seven. Although parents should not expect their two-and-a-half-year-olds to conserve as they participate in this activity, many seem to enjoy this kind of play anyway.

Questions Keep Coming

This is the time your child will be asking many questions, and family photos are likely to stimulate interesting ones.

Materials

Family photo album

Behind the Scenes

Questions are plentiful at this stage, and providing a venue for encouraging them is good for both of you.

Research Roundup!

Curiosity plays a major role in the lives of preschoolers, according to a study conducted by researchers Brandy Frazier, Susan Gellman, and Henry Wellman. The reason young children ask so many *why* questions stems from a genuine desire for an explanation. The researchers carried out two studies of two- to five-year-olds, focusing on their *how* and *why* questions, as well as their requests for explanatory information, and looked carefully at the children's reactions to the answers they received from adults. Results showed that the children seemed to be more satisfied when they received an explanatory answer than when they did not. They were also more likely to repeat their original question or provide their own alternative reason when they didn't hear an explanatory response.

How to Do It

1. Go through the photo album, asking questions such as:

   - Who is in the picture?
   - What is he doing?
   - Where do you think they are going?
   - When was the party, trip, or visit . . . ?
   - Why do you think he did that?

2. Take turns asking questions about the pictures.

Describing

With tantrums on the way out, word articulation is becoming important for your child's development. This is a wonderful time for your child to practice making herself clear in conversation.

Materials
5 safe and interesting objects

Behind the Scenes
This activity is a good reminder of how important you are to your child as a model in every way. Your speech is very important in helping her articulate her thoughts. It is the training language for her development.

Research Roundup!
Speech-language pathologist Dorothy P. Dougherty offers suggestions for modeling correct speech for your child:

- Speak clearly, naturally, and correctly. Establish eye contact and speak at an easy-to-understand rate.

- Model the correct way to say a word. If your child says a word incorrectly, say the word correctly and give your child opportunity to say it back to you correctly.

- Repeat a troublesome word and overenunciate the difficult sound by saying it louder and longer. Continue talking and make the word a natural part of your conversation.

- Give your child many opportunities to hear hard sounds pronounced correctly. This will make it easier for her to hear the difference between correct and incorrect pronunciations, and it will also make it easier to say the sound when she is ready.

Reading Time VII

You can share a lot of information with your child through reading books together. The more time you spend reading together, the higher the quality and quantity of your teaching.

Materials

Children's book

How to Do It

1. Choose any book you wish that tells a story, teaches a lesson, or provides information on a given topic. Be sure to pick one that is on the preschool level.

2. As you read, stop to point to pictures and talk about them.

3. Ask your child questions about what is happening.

4. Ask other questions that do not have a right or wrong answer, but that will help you figure out how well she understands the content.

5. Do not wait long for an answer. Tell her your thoughts freely. It is important that this be a sharing, nurturing experience, not one that puts your child on the spot.

6. If your child asks a question, answer it by asking the same question back to her. Many times children ask questions so that they can answer them. If that is not the case, answer your child by repeating the question and answering it after a pause. Here is an example:

   Child: Where is the boy?
   You: Where is the boy?

7. If your child does not answer right away, you answer.

   You: The boy is behind the tree.

Behind the Scenes

There are books on the preschool level covering a wide range of topics. Choose books that you think will be of special interest to your child. If you aren't sure which books to choose, your local librarian will be a great resource.

Research Roundup!

According to guidance from the U.S. Department of Education's website, children's brains grow as they learn, and by the end of those important first three years of life, the more they have learned, the larger their brains and the better prepared they will be to become readers. A process in the earliest years that includes reading, singing, and talking to children is the foundation for future learning.

Self-Esteem Flourishes

Follow Me

When you follow your child, you will be helping her to feel good inside. You will know exactly what this means when you have your child follow you.

Materials
None

Behind the Scenes
Your child spends an exorbitant amount of time doing what others tell her to do. This opportunity to be on the opposite end of the spectrum as leader will bring her great pride and joy.

Research Roundup!
Playing Follow the Leader encourages children to listen, according to writer Joey Papa in the article "Follow-the-Leader Children's Games." It is also a fun way to connect with children while teaching them to follow directions. While this activity contributes much to self-esteem development, it also benefits cognitive, motor, social-emotional, and language development.

How to Do It

1. Take turns saying, "Follow me" and then go into a different room. To add fun and excitement to your game, pretend you are off to find something of a particular color. Then when you find it, stop and say something like, "Look, I found it!"

2. Encourage your child to pick a color and lead you to seek a different object. Surprise is part of this play.

Dancing Fun

Dancing to music is great fun. Turning that dancing into a performance makes for an even more valuable activity. Dancing for an audience brings more positive attention for your child.

Materials
Music of your choice

Behind the Scenes
Your two-and-a-half-year-old probably likes dancing any time or place. Giving her your undivided attention while she is performing shows that you value this activity.

How to Do It

1. Play any music you like.

2. Take turns dancing to the music.

3. Designate a chair to sit in while you each watch the other one perform.

4. Invite family members or close friends to join your dancing fun!

Research Roundup!

"Dance is a powerful ally for developing many of the attributes of a growing child," according to the National Dance Education Organization. Because children like to move and express feelings, and because it comes naturally, it makes sense to include dance in early childhood education. As with many other activities, dance is somewhat misunderstood. While it appears to be simply a physical activity, the reality is that dance has cognitive, social-emotional, language, and self-esteem benefits that far outweigh the physical benefits.

Computer Time II

This activity builds on any computer exposure you have already given your child. Now you can have fun with the keyboard.

Materials

Computer

Behind the Scenes

This kind of play is structured and provides an excellent way for you to expose your child to language and basic technology skills. By adding important information about handling this kind of equipment with proper care, you are crediting your child with being responsible. That will make her feel valued.

Research Roundup!

The American Academy of Pediatrics recommends that children under two should have no screen time beyond video chats, but at age two, some exposure may be beneficial. As our world becomes more digitally driven, children will need to learn how to type, in addition to learning handwriting skills. There are many free educational typing applications available for use on the computer or smart device, but use should be limited to an hour or less. PBS's Child Development Tracker says that two-year-old children can benefit from computer time and develop more language skills due to several factors, including the following:

- Two-year-olds are highly curious.

- New discoveries are facilitated by their blossoming language skills that prompt many *why*, *what*, and *how* questions.

How to Do It

1. Open your word processing program.

2. On a blank document, set the font size to 16.

3. Teach your child how to press keys that will write her name.

4. Add other words as you like. If you get to simple sentences, here are some suggestions:

   - I like you.

   - You can smile.

   - Clap your hands.

5. Print out whatever words or sentences you wish.

6. Be sure not to leave your child unattended at any time during your computer play.

- They can say and understand hundreds of words.

- They understand simple directions.

- Children this age are laying the groundwork for reading and writing.

Look at Me

Hearing words used properly helps children learn the meaning of words. Acting them out makes them even more memorable.

Materials

None

Behind the Scenes

Any kind of acting is a learning experience for a child, but as your child acts in front of you, the learning power is expanded. Your attention will make your child feel good and make the learning process more meaningful. Taking turns also adds to the effectiveness because it sends the message to your child about the value of sharing the learning experience.

Research Roundup!

PBS's Child Development Tracker details excellent descriptions of two-year-olds. While the website refers to all kinds of skills, the following points support activities that encourage actions and motions of all kinds.

How to Do It

1. Move your body and describe your movements to your child, such as "I raise my arms over my head. I put my arms down."

2. Ask your two-and-a-half-year-old to copy your movements.

3. Once your child catches on, she can move her body and you can copy her. Here are a few examples:

   - I am small. Now I'm tall.
   - I sit down. Now I stand.
   - I jump. Now I clap.

- Two-year-olds enjoy using their senses and motor skills to explore the world.

- Children this age pretend more during play.

- They pick up most parts of speech to form more complete sentences.

- They understand simple directions.

- They make sounds by banging and shaking instruments and household items.

Record-a-Story

Your child will especially love having a story recorded by you. It will be great to listen to together while you are at home and even better for times when you are away. After hearing many repetitions of the story, she may begin to recognize some of the words in print.

Materials
Drinking glass
Metal spoon
Children's book

Behind the Scenes
Books are good, and recorded books are excellent, but there is no reading experience for your child that will be quite like having a book recorded by you. Anything that you can individualize for your child on your recording will add to her joy. Saying her name and adding a special message will increase the effectiveness of this learning experience and boost your child's self-esteem at the same time.

Research Roundup!
An attentive parent-child relationship, according to the Encyclopedia on Early Childhood Development, has a major positive influence on most aspects of child development. "High self-esteem, advanced school achievement, and high-functioning cognitive development and behavior" are most noted in children who have had this kind of effective parenting. Dr. Susan H. Landry finds that "cognitive and social skills needed for later success in school are best supported by a parenting style known as responsive parenting." This responsiveness is characterized by strong verbal communication and paying attention to and expanding on the child's interests.

Epilogue: The Power of the Parent

When your baby came into the world, someone else was born at the same time and that was you as a parent. You may not even have known how to hold a newborn. You were probably a little afraid of the whole idea. That all changed, however, and you learned how to do that and more. Newborns are delicate and need great care, and it is not just anyone who can give it. This point becomes even clearer when you notice you are not quite sure how to hold someone else's baby.

Another interesting aspect of becoming a parent is that your baby knows who you are as well. Your little one prefers that you hold him. You two get to know each other better every day with every interaction, no matter how small.

Carrying your baby is another changing phenomenon. Each day your baby grows and gets ever-so-slightly heavier, and at the same time you grow in strength to be able to hold him. A friend or a grandparent can try to pick up your little one and may find it difficult, and you will likely think it is easy.

This concept of incremental weight is similar to the gradual developmental growth of your child. Through very small steps, your little one grows through ages and stages. The changes occur slowly, steadily, and right before your eyes, but they are hard to see with daily interaction. With that in mind, the selected activities in this book are sensitive to this growth and are designed to help you enjoy your child.

Every minute, every hour, and every day are important in the life of your child, especially in the early years. Every experience affects every one that follows. The process can be compared to cutting paths. Picture a field of beautifully cut grass. One walker crosses it one way, and another one goes in a different direction. Everyone finds his own way. So it is with the experiences that build your child's brain. All that a baby sees, hears, tastes, touches, and smells make up the experiences that form brain paths. The repeated ones become the strongest. If most of the experiences in the early days are positive, you will see your baby growing up in productive ways. However, if most of them in one way or another are not, you will see negative behavior. Heredity factors play a major role in how your child will grow, but environmental input is critical.

For a child to be ready to start school at age four or five, she needs to be exposed to the finest early experiences in the first three years. For a child to have those, every parent needs to know how to provide them. While this is a comprehensive process that takes place over time, playing with your child is very important.

I wish you many happy hours of playing and learning with your child.

References

Addyman, Caspar, and Ishbel Addyman. 2013. "The Science of Baby Laughter," *Comedy Studies* 4(2): 143–153.

Ainsworth, Mary D. S., et al. 1978. *Patterns of Attachment: A Psychological Study of the Strange Situation*. Hillsdale, NJ: Erlbaum.

American Academy of Pediatrics, "American Academy of Pediatrics Announces New Recommendations for Children's Media Use," news release on October 21, 2016. https://www.aap.org/en-us/about-the-aap/aap-press-room/pages/american-academy-of-pediatrics-announces-new-recommendations-for-childrens-media-use.aspx

American Academy of Pediatrics. 2015. "Cognitive Development: Two-Year-Old." Healthy Children. https://www.healthychildren.org/English/ages-stages/toddler/Pages/Cognitive-Development-Two-Year-Old.aspx

American Academy of Pediatrics. 2015. "Is Your Baby's Physical Development on Track?" Healthy Children. https://www.healthychildren.org/English/ages-stages/baby/Pages/Is-Your-Babys-Physical-Development-on-Track.aspx

American Academy of Pediatrics. 2015. "Language Development: 2-Year-Olds." Healthy Children. https://www.healthychildren.org/English/ages-stages/toddler/Pages/Language-Development-2-Year-Olds.aspx

American Academy of Pediatrics. 2015. "Safety for Your Child: 2 to 4 Years." Healthy Children. https://www.healthychildren.org/English/ages-stages/toddler/Pages/Safety-for-Your-Child-2-to-4-Years.aspx

American Academy of Pediatrics. 2009. *Caring for Your Baby and Young Child: Birth to Age 5*. New York: Bantam.

American Academy of Pediatrics. 2003. "Eye Examination in Infants, Children, and Young Adults by Pediatricians." *Pediatrics* 111(4). http://pediatrics.aappublications.org/content/111/4/902

American Optometric Association Foundation. n.d. "InfantSEE." American Optometric Association Foundation. http://www.infantsee.org/

Anthony, Michelle. n.d. "Early Literacy: Writing with 0–2 Year Olds." Scholastic Parents. http://www.scholastic.com/parents/resources/article/early-literacy-writing-0-2-year-olds

Ask Dr. Sears. n.d. "12 Ways to Raise a Confident Child." Ask Dr. Sears. https://www.askdrsears.com/topics/parenting/child-rearing-and-development/12-ways-help-your-child-build-self-confidence

Ask Dr. Sears. n.d. "25 Ways to Talk So Children Will Listen." Ask Dr. Sears. https://www.askdrsears.com/topics/parenting/discipline-behavior/25-ways-talk-so-children-will-listen

Azar, Beth. 2002. "The Power of Pretending." *Monitor on Psychology* 33(3): 46.

Baby Centre. n.d. "Throwing and Catching: Toddler Development." Baby Centre. https://www.babycentre.co.uk/a556927/throwing-and-catching-toddler-development

Balmain, Melissa. n.d. "Boost Your Baby's Self-Esteem." Parenting. http://www.parenting.com/article/boost-your-babys-self-esteem

Balmain, Melissa. 2008. "How to Raise a Confident Kid." CNN.com. http://www.cnn.com/2008/HEALTH/family/09/08/parenting.confidence/index.html

Beaty, J. J. 2014. "Early Writing and Scribbling." Education.com. https://www.education.com/reference/article/early-writing-scribbling/

Benasich, April, et al. 2014. "Plasticity in Developing Brain: Active Auditory Exposure Impacts Prelinguistic Acoustic Mapping" *Journal of Neuroscience* 34(40): 13349-13363.

Bergelson, Elika, and Daniel Swingley. 2011. "At 6-9 Months, Human Infants Know the Meanings of Many Common Nouns" *Proceedings of the National Academy of Sciences*. http://www.pnas.org/content/109/9/3253

Bergelson, Elika, and Daniel Swingley. 2014. "Early Word Comprehension in Infants: Replication and Extension." *Language Learning and Development* 11(4): 369-380.

Berman, Jenn. n.d. "10 Reasons Play Makes Babies Smarter." Parenting.com. http://www.parenting.com/article/why-play-makes-babies-smarter

Bhattacharjee, Yudhijit. 2015. "Baby Brains: The First Year." National Georgraphic. http://ngm.nationalgeographic.com/2015/01/baby-brains/bhattacharjee-text

Borchard, Therese. 2013. "Words Can Change Your Brain." Everyday Health. http://www.everydayhealth.com/columns/therese-borchard-sanity-break/420/

Boris, Neil, Michael Fueyo, and Charles Zenah. 1997. "The Clinical Assessment of Attachment in Children Under Five." *Journal of the American Academy of Adolescent Psychiatry* 36(2): 291-293.

Boys Town National Research Hospital. n.d. "Giving Your Child Positive Attention." Boys Town National Research Hospital. https://www.babyhearing.org/parenting/positive-attention

Brown, Stephanie. 2017. "Why Your Child Should Be Playing with Balls." Very Well. https://www.verywell.com/why-your-child-should-be-playing-with-balls-289705

Cacola, Priscila, et al. 2015. "Further Development and Validation of the Affordance in the Home Environment for Motor Development-Infant Scale (AHEMD-IS)." *Physical Therapy* 95(6): 901-923.

Carey, Bjorn. 2013. "Talking Directly to Toddlers Strengthens Their Language Skills, Stanford Research Shows." Stanford News. http://news.stanford.edu/news/2013/october/fernald-vocab-development-101513.html

Carter, Mildred, and Tammy Weber. 1983. *Body Reflexology: Healing at Your Fingertips*. New York: Reward Books of the Penguin Group.

The Center for Parenting Education. n.d. "Responsibility and Chores: Part I: Benefits of Chores." The Center for Parenting Education. http://centerforparentingeducation.org/library-of-articles/responsibility-and-chores/part-i-benefits-of-chores/

Centre of Excellence for Early Childhood Development (CEECD) and the Strategic Knowledge Cluster on Early Child Development (SKC-ECD). 2011. "Physical Activity in Early Childhood: Setting the Stage for Lifelong Healthy Habits." http://www.excellence-earlychildhood.ca/documents/parenting_2011-04.pdf

Child & Family Development. 2013. "Is Your Child Struggling to Walk Up or Down Stairs?" Child & Family Development. http://www.childandfamilydevelopment.com/blog/2013/05/03/is-your-child-struggling-to-walk-up-or-down-stairs

Child Development Institute. n.d. "Forms of Play." Child Development Institute. https://childdevelopmentinfo.com/child-development/play-work-of-children/pl3

Children's Therapy and Family Resource Centre. n.d. "Infant Developmental Milestones." Children's Therapy and Family Resource Centre. http://www.kamloopschildrenstherapy.org/fine-motor-skills-infant-milestons

Childress, Dana. 2013. "Peek-A-Boo—Strategies to Teach Object Permanence." Early Intervention Strategies for Success blog. http://veipd.org/earlyintervention/2013/03/21/peek-a-boo-strategies-to-teach-object-permanence/

Clark, Jane E. 2007. "On the Problem of Motor Skill Development." *Journal of Physical Education, Recreation, and Dance* 78(5): 39-44.

Cochran, Sylvia. 2012. "A Guide to Fun and Easy Sorting Activities for Toddlers." Bright Hub Education. http://www.brighthubeducation.com/toddler-activities-learning/34774-simple-sorting-activities-for-toddlers/

Colorado Department of Education. n.d. "Bubbles and Toddlers." Colorado Department of Education. https://www.cde.state.co.us/cdelib/bubblesfortoddlers

Common Sense Media. 2017. "The Common Sense Census: Media Use by Kids Age 0 to 8." Common Sense Media. https://www.commonsensemedia.org/research/the-common-sense-census-media-use-by-kids-age-zero-to-eight-2017

Connolly, Maureen. 2007. "Your Baby: 10 Milestones for the First 2 Years." CNN. http://www.cnn.com/2007/HEALTH/parenting/06/07/par.baby.milestones/

Davis, Janice. 2012. "Why Are Puzzles So Important for Kids Learning?" Learning4Kids. http://www.learning4kids.net/2012/02/21/why-are-puzzles-so-good-for-kids-learning/

DeBenedet, Anthony T., and Lawrence J. Cohen. 2011. *The Art of Roughhousing: Good Old-Fashioned Horseplay and Why Every Kid Needs It.* Philadelphia, PA: Quirk Books.

Decarr, Kristen. 2016. "Parents Increase Kids' Attention Span with Focus on Shared Objects." Education News. http://www.educationnews.org/parenting/parents-increase-kids-attention-span-with-focus-on-shared-objects/

Dewar, Gwen. 2016. "Why Toy Blocks Rock: The Science of Building and Construction Toys." Parenting Science. http://www.parentingscience.com/toy-blocks.html

Donahue, Jennifer. 2008. "Toys that Encourage Creative Play." ParentMap. https://www.parentmap.com/article/toys-that-encourage-creative-play

Dougherty, Dorothy. n.d. "Speech and Language Problems: Seven Ways to Help Your Child Speak Clearly." Parent Guide News. http://www.parentguidenews.com/Articles/SpeechandLanguageProblems

Duncan, et al. 2007. "School Readiness and Later Achievement." Developmental Psychology 43(6): 1428-1446.

Eckersley, Sian. 2013. "Mouth Activities." Occupational Therapy for Children. http://occupationaltherapyforchildren.over-blog.com/article-mouth-activities-118113011.html

Encyclopedia on Early Childhood Development. 2011. "Physical Activity in Early Childhood: Setting the Stage for Lifelong Healthy Habits." Encyclopedia on Early Childhood Development. http://www.excellence-earlychildhood.ca/documents/parenting_2011-04.pdf

Erikson, Erik. 1950. *Childhood and Society.* New York: Norton.

Extension.org. 2015. "The Block Center in Child Care." Extension.org. http://articles.extension.org/pages/67335/the-block-center-in-child-care

Extension.org. 2015. "Using Puppets in Child Care." Extension.org. http://articles.extension.org/pages/67243/using-puppets-in-child-care

Farroni, Teresa, et al. 2002. "Eye Contact Detection in Humans From Birth." *Proceedings of the National Academy of Science of the United States of America* 99(14): 9602–9605.

Fernald, Anne, Amy Perfors, and Virginia Marchman. 2006. "Picking Up Speed in Understanding: Speech Processing Efficiency and Vocabulary Growth Across the 2nd Year." *Developmental Psychology* 42(1):98-116.

Field, Tiffany, Miguel Diego, and Maria Hernandez-Reif. 2007. "Massage Therapy Research." *Developmental Review* 27(1): 75–89.

Fox, Robin. n.d. "Food and Eating: An Anthropological Perspective." Social Issues Research Centre. http://www.sirc.org/publik/foxfood.pdf

Frazier, Brandy, Susan Gelman, and Henry Wellman. 2009. "Preschoolers' Search for Explanatory Information Within Adult-Child Conversation." *Child Development* 80(6): 1592.

Geller, David. n.d. "How Can I Teach My Child to Hit, Kick, and Catch a Ball?" Baby Center. https://www.babycenter.com/404_how-can-i-teach-my-child-to-hit-kick-and-catch-a-ball_6881.bc

Gillespie, Linda. 2009. "Why Do Babies Like Boxes Best?" *Young Children* 64(3): 48-49.

Gervain, Judit, et al. 2008. "The Neonate Brain Detects Speech Structure." *Proceedings of the National Academy of Science of the United States of America* 105(37): 14222-14227.

Goldberg, Sally. 2002. *Constructive Parenting.* Boston, MA: Allyn and Bacon.

Goldberg, Sally. 2001. *Baby and Toddler Learning Fun.* Cambridge, MA: Perseus.

Goldberg, Sally. 1997. *Parent Involvement Begins at Birth.* Needham Heights, MA: Allyn and Bacon.

Goldberg, Sally. 1981. *Teaching with Toys.* Ann Arbor, MI: University of Michigan Press.

Gonzalez-Mena, Janet. 2007. "What to Do for a Fussy Baby: A Problem-Solving Approach." *Young Children* 62(5): 20–24.

Granitur, Eric. 1996. *I Love You Daddy: Thoughts from a Father.* Miami Beach, FL: Sydney's Sproutin' Company.

Greenberg, Jan. 2012. "More, All Gone, Empty, Full: Math Talk Every Day in Every Way." *Young Children* 67(3): 62-64.

Grissmer, David W., et al. 2010. "Fine Motor Skills and Early Comprehension of the World: Two New School Readiness Indicators." *Developmental Psychology* 46(5): 1008-1017.

Gross, Carol M. 2012. "Science Concepts Young Children Learn through Water Play." *Dimensions of Early Childhood* 40(2): 3-12.

Gunner, Kathy B., et al. 2005. "Health Promotion Strategies to Encourage Physical Activity in Infants, Toddlers, and Preschoolers." *Journal of Pediatric Health Care* 19(4): 253-258.

Guyton, Gabriel. 2011. "Using Toys to Support Development Infant-Toddler Learning and Development," Young Children 66(5): 50-54.

Hallam, Susan. 2010. "The Power of Music: Its Impact on the Intellectual, Social, and Personal Development of Children and Young People." *International Journal of Music Education* 28(3): 269-289.

Harmon, Katherine. 2010. "How Important Is Physical Contact with Your Infant?" *Scientific American.* https://www.scientificamerican.com/article/infant-touch/

Harper, Laurie J. 2011. "Nursery Rhyme Knowledge and Phonological Awareness in Preschool Children." *The Journal of Language and Literacy Education* 7(1): 65–78.

Heath, Shirley Brice. 1982. "What No Bedtime Story Means: Narrative Skills at Home and at School." *Language in Society* 11(1): 49-76.

Hoecker, Jay. n.d. "Should I Be Concerned That My Two-Year-Old Doesn't Say Many Words and Is Hard to Understand?" Infant Toddler Health, Mayo Clinic. http://www.mayoclinic.org/healthy-lifestyle/infant-and-toddler-health/expert-answers/toddler-speech-development/faq-20057847

Henry, Sarah. 2016. "How to Build Your Preschooler's Self-Esteem." Baby Center. https://www.babycenter.com/0_how-to-build-your-preschoolers-self-esteem_64036.bc

Herbert, Jane S., Julien Gross, and Harlene Hayn. 2006. "Age-Related Changes in Deferred Imitation Between 6 and 9 Months of Age." *Infant Behavior and Development* 29(1): 136-139.

Hirshon, Bob. n.d. "Bouncing Babies." American Association for the Advancement of Science. http://sciencenetlinks.com/science-news/science-updates/bouncing-babies/

Holland, Jeanne W. 2008. "Reading Aloud with Infants: The Controversy, the Myth, and a Case Study." *Early Childhood Education Journal* 35(4): 383-385.

Honig, Alice. 2010. "Keys to Quality Infant/Toddler Care: Nurturing Baby's Life Journey." *Young Children* 65(5): 40–47.

How Kids Develop. 2008. "Childhood Development: 2 to 3 Years." How Kids Develop. http://www.howkidsdevelop.com/2-3years. html

Huitt, William G., and Courtney Dawson. 2011. "Social Development: Why It is Important and How to Impact It." *Educational Psychology Interactive*. Valdosta, GA: Valdosta State University. www.edpsycinteractive.org/papers/socdev.pdf

Infant and Toddler Forum. 2013. "Physical Activity and Play for Toddlers." Infant and Toddler Forum. https://www.infantandtoddlerforum.org/media/upload/pdf-downloads/3.4_Physical_Activity_and_Play.pdf

Indiana University. 2008. "New Thoughts on Language Acquisition: Toddlers as Data Miners." Science Daily. https://www.sciencedaily.com/releases/2008/01/080129215316.htm

Institute of Medicine. 2000. *From Neurons to Neighborhoods: The Science of Early Childhood Development*. Washington, DC: The National Academies Press.

Jensen, Eric. 2005. *Teaching with the Brain in Mind*. 2nd ed. Alexandria, VA: ASCD.

JRank. n.d. "Hand-Eye Coordination: Toddlerhood, Preschool Years, School-aged Children. JRank. http://psychology.jrank.org/pages/294/Hand-Eye-Coordination.html

Kaufman, Scott Barry. 2013. "The Real Neuroscience of Creativity." *Scientific American*. https://blogs.scientificamerican.com/beautiful-minds/the-real-neuroscience-of-creativity/

Kaufman, Scott Barry. 2012. "10 Insights to Enhance the Joy of Learning." *Psychology Today*. https://www.psychologytoday.com/blog/beautiful-minds/201208/10-insights-enhance-the-joy-learning

KBYU Eleven. 2010. "The Brain: How Children Develop." KBYU Eleven. http://www.kbyutv.org/kidsandfamily/readytolearn/file.axd?file=2011%2F3%2F5+The+Brain.pdf

Kear, Nicole. 2017. "Teaching a Toddler to Follow Directions." Parenting. http://www.parenting.com/article/teaching-a-toddler-to-follow-directions

Kidd, Celeste, Steven T. Piantadosi, and Richard N. Aslin. 2012. "The Goldilocks Effect: Human Infants Allocate Attention to Visual Sequences That Are Neither Too Simple Nor Too Complex." *PLoS One*. http://journals.plos.org/plosone/article?id=10.1371/journal.pone.0036399

Kopko, Kimberly. n.d. "Research Sheds Light on How Babies Learn and Develop Language." Cornell University College of Human Development, Outreach, and Extension. http://www.human.cornell.edu/hd/outreach-extension/upload/casasola.pdf

Koralek, Derry. 2015. "Ten Things Children Learn from Block Play." *Young Children* 70(1).

Kuhl, Patricia K. 2011. "Early Language Learning and Literacy: Neuroscience Implications for Education." *Mind, Brain, and Education* 5(3):128-142.

Landry, Susan. 2014. "The Role of Parents in Early Childhood Learning." Encyclopedia on Early Childhood Development. http://www.child-encyclopedia.com/parenting-skills/according-experts/role-parents-early-childhood-learning

Lao, Joseph. 2017. "Infant Language Development." Parenting Literacy. http://www.parentingliteracy.com/parenting-a-z/45-mental-development/97-infant-language-development

Leach, Penelope. 2010. *Your Baby & Child: From Birth to Age Five*. New York: Knopf.

Leong, Deborah J., and Elena Bodrova. 2012. "Assessing and Scaffolding: Make-Believe Play." *Young Children* 67(1): 28–34. https://www.naeyc.org/files/yc/file/201201/Leong_Make_Believe_Play_Jan2012.pdf

Leong, Victoria, et al. 2017. "Speaker Gaze Increases Information Coupling Between Infant and Adult Brains." *Proceedings of the National Academy of Sciences* 114(50): 13290-13295.

Levitin, Daniel. 2007. *This Is Your Brain on Music*. New York: Penguin.

Liberman, Zoe, et al. 2016. "Early Emerging System for Reasoning about the Social Nature of Food." *Proceedings of the National Academy of Sciences* 113(34): 9480-9485.

Live Science. 2012. "Why Are 'Mama' and 'Dada' a Baby's First Words?" Live Science. https://www.livescience.com/32191-why-are-mama-and-dada-a-babys-first-words.html

Loewenberg, Aaron. 2015. "New Research: Two-Year-Old Vocabulary Predicts Kindergarten Success." New America. https://www.newamerica.org/education-policy/edcentral/vocabstudy/

Lowry, Lauren. n.d. "What Makes Your Child 'Tick'? Using Children's Interests to Build Communication Skills." The Hanen Centre. http://www.hanen.org/helpful-info/articles/what-makes-your-child-tick-.aspx

Martinez, Eliza. n.d. "Manipulative Play Activities for Toddlers." Our Everyday Life. http://oureverydaylife.com/manipulative-play-activities-toddlers-1476.html

McKay, Liesa. 2017. "Out of Sight, Out of Mind: The Development of Object Permanence." Intellidance. http://blog.intellidance.ca/blog/8-10-2011/out-sight-out-mind-development-object-permanence

McLeod, Saul. 2010. "Concrete Operational Stages." Simply Psychology. https://www.simplypsychology.org/concrete-operational.html

Micco, Nicci. n.d. "12 Fun Baby Learning Games." Parenting. http://www.parenting.com/article/baby-learning-activities

Miller, Lori Kase. 2014. "The Benefits of Introducing Baby to Music," *Parents Magazine*. http://www.parents.com/baby/development/intellectual/rock-the-cradle/

Moore, Kimberly. 2011. "Does Singing to Your Baby Really Work?" *Psychology Today*. https://www.psychologytoday.com/blog/your-musical-self/201107/does-singing-your-baby-really-work

Morin, Amanda. n.d. "Developmental Milestones for Typical 2-Year-Olds." Understood.org. https://www.understood.org/en/learning-attention-issues/signs-symptoms/developmental-milestones/developmental-milestones-for-typical-2-year-olds

Morin, Amanda. n.d. "The Importance of Self-Awareness for Kids with Learning and Attention Issues." Understood for Learning and Attention Issues. https://www.understood.org/en/friends-feelings/empowering-your-child/self-awareness/the-importance-of-self-awareness

Morin, Amy. 2016. "Positive Attention Reduces Behavioral Problems: Daily 'Time In' Can Reduce the Need for 'Time Out.'" Very Well. https://www.verywell.com/positive-attention-reduces-behavioral-problems-1094784

Moss, Kate. 2005. "Some Things to Learn from Learning through Touch." Texas School for the Blind and Visually Impaired. http://www.tsbvi.edu/seehear/spring05/things.htm

NAEYC for Families. n.d. "Playdough Power." NAEYC. https://www.naeyc.org/our-work/families/playdough-power

Narvaez, Darcia. 2011. "Where are the Happy Babies?" *Psychology Today*. https://www.psychologytoday.com/blog/moral-landscapes/201108/where-are-the-happy-babies

National Dance Education Organization. 2017. "Standards for Dance in Early Childhood." NDEO. http://www.ndeo.org/content.aspx?page_id=22&club_id=893257&module_id=55411

National Institute of Child Health and Human Development. n.d. Safe to Sleep. https://www1.nichd.nih.gov/sts/Pages/default.aspx

National Institutes of Health. 2013. "Shape Your Family's Habits: Helping Kids Make Healthy Choices." NIH News in Health. https://newsinhealth.nih.gov/issue/feb2013/feature1

Nemours. n.d. "Fitness and Your 2- to 3-Year-Old." KidsHealth. http://kidshealth.org/en/parents/fitness-2-3.html

Newberg, Andrew, and Mark Robert Waldman. 2012. *Words Can Change Your Brain: 12 Conversation Strategies to Build Trust, Resolve Conflict, and Increase Intimacy*. New York: Avery.

Nierenberg, Cari. 2016. "Simple Trick May Improve an Infant's Attention Span." Live Science. https://www.livescience.com/54594-tips-to-improve-infants-attention-span.html

Niland, Amanda. 2015. "Row, Row, Row Your Boat: Singing, Identity, and Belonging in a Nursery." *International Journal of Early Years Education* 23(1): 4-16.

Northport-East Northport Public Library. n.d. "Road to Reading." Northport-East Northport Public Library. http://www.nenpl.org/childrens/programs/roadtoreading.php

Pantell, Robert, et al. 2002. *Taking Care of Your Child: A Parent's Guide to Complete Medical Care.* Boston, MA: Da Capo Press.

Papa, Joey. n.d. "Follow-the-Leader Children's Games." Our Everyday Life. https://oureverydaylife.com/followtheleader-childrens-games-5811204.html

Parlakian, Rebecca, and Claire Lerner. 2007. "Promoting Healthy Eating Habits Right from the Start," *Beyond the Journal: Young Children on the Web.* http://va.gapitc.org/wp-content/uploads/2012/11/3-RockingandRolling.pdf

Patsalides, Laurie. 2012. "Infant-Toddler Development with Daycare Mirrors." Bright Hub Education. http://www.brighthubeducation.com/toddler-activities-learning/101124-mirrors-as-a-developmental-tool/

Petersen, Sandra, Emily J. Adams, and Linda Gillespie. 2016. "Rocking and Rolling: Learning to Move." *Young Children* 71(5).

PBS Parents. n.d. "Child Development Tracker: Your Two-Year-Old." PBS Parents. http://www.pbs.org/parents/childdevelopmenttracker/two/index.html

Piaget, Louis. 1977. *The Development of Thought: Equilibration of Cognitive Structures.* New York: Viking.

Pierce, Patsy, ed. n.d. *Baby Power: A Guide for Families for Using Assistive Technology With Their Infants and Toddlers.* Chapel Hill, NC: The Center for Literacy and Disabilities Studies. http://www2.edc.org/ncip/library/ec/power.htm

Play and Playground Encyclopedia. n.d. "Open-Ended Play." Play and Playground Encyclopedia. https://pgpedia.com/o/open-ended-play

Raising Children Network. 2017. "Building Self-Esteem: Babies and Children." Raising Children. http://raisingchildren.net.au/articles/self-esteem_different_ages.html

Raising Children Network. 2015. "Teaching Your Child How to Get Dressed." Raising Children. http://raisingchildren.net.au/articles/getting_dressed.html

Reading Rockets. n.d. "Print Awareness." Reading Rockets. http://www.readingrockets.org/teaching/reading-basics/printawareness

Reading Rockets. 2007. "Nursery Rhymes: Not Just for Babies!" Reading Rockets. http://www.readingrockets.org/article/nursery-rhymes-not-just-babies

Roberts, Michelle. 2005. "Babies 'Have Favorite Colours.'" BBC News. http://news.bbc.co.uk/2/hi/health/4474725.stm

Scholastic. n.d. "All About Blocks." Scholastic. http://www.scholastic.com/parents/resources/article/creativity-play/all-about-blocks

School Sparks. n.d. "Fine Motor Development." School Sparks. http://www.schoolsparks.com/early-childhood-development/fine-motor

Science Daily. 2015. "Two-Year-Olds with Poor Language Skills Fall Behind at Play." Science Daily. https://www.sciencedaily.com/releases/2015/11/151110083123.htm

Science NetLinks. n.d. "Bouncing Babies." Science NetLinks. http://sciencenetlinks.com/science-news/science-updates/bouncing-babies/

Seefeldt, Carol, and Barbara Wasik. 2010. "Cognitive Development of Preschoolers." Education. https://www.education.com/reference/article/cognitive-development-preschoolers/

Seo, Kyoung-Hye, and Herbert Ginsburg. 2004. "What Is Developmentally Appropriate in Early Childhood Mathematics Education? Lessons from New Research." In Engaging Young Children in Mathematics. Hillsdale, NJ: Lawrence Erlbaum.

Sizer, Michael. n.d. "The Surprising Meaning and Benefits of Nursery Rhymes." PBS.org. http://www.pbs.org/parents/education/reading-language/reading-tips/the-surprising-meaning-and-benefits-of-nursery-rhymes/

Snow, Catherine E. 1977. "The Development of Conversation Between Mothers and Babies." *Journal of Child Language* 4:1-22.

Society for Research in Child Development. 2009. "When Preschoolers Ask Questions, They Want Explanations." Science Daily. https://www.sciencedaily.com/releases/2009/11/091113083254.htm

Stahl, Aimee E., and Lisa Feigenson. 2015. "Observing the Unexpected Enhances Infants' Learning and Exploration." *Science* 348 (6230): 91–94.

Stamm, Jill. 2016. *Boosting Brain Power: 52 Ways to Use What Science Tells Us.* Lewisville, NC: Gryphon House.

Stiefel, Chana. n.d. "What Your Child Learns By Imitating You." Parents. http://www.parents.com/toddlers-preschoolers/development/behavioral/learning-by-imitating-you/

Supporting Success for Children with Hearing Loss. n.d. "Self-Concept: Infants, Toddlers, Preschoolers." Supporting Success for Children with Hearing Loss. http://successforkidswithhearingloss.com/for-professionals/self-concept-infants-to-preschoolers/

Teaching Strategies. 2010. "Research Foundation: Mathematics." Teaching Strategies. https://teachingstrategies.com/wp-content/uploads/2017/03/Research-Foundation-Math.pdf

University of California at San Diego School of Medicine, Child and Adolescent Services Research Center. 2008. "Childhood Development: 2 to 3 Years." How Kids Develop. http://www.howkidsdevelop.com/2-3years.html

University of Maryland Medical Center. n.d. "Infant Reflexes." University of Maryland Medical Center. http://www.umm.edu/Health/Medical/Ency/Articles/Infant-reflexes

University of Missouri Extension. n.d. "Building Strong Families: Kids and Self-Esteem." University of Missouri Extension. http://extension.missouri.edu/bsf/selfesteem/index.htm

University of Rochester Medical Center. 2017. "Toddler/Preschooler Safety Tips." University of Rochester Medical Center, Golisano Children's Hospital. https://www.urmc.rochester.edu/childrens-hospital/safety/age-tips/toddler-safety.aspx

University of Texas at Arlington. 2015. "Household Items, Toys Key to Infant Motor Skill Development, Research Finds," Science Daily. https://www.sciencedaily.com/releases/2015/06/150604100913.htm

Urban Child Institute. 2012. "Enhancing Development Through the Sense of Touch." Urban Child Institute. http://www.urbanchildinstitute.org/articles/research-to-policy/research/enhancing-development-through-the-sense-of-touch

Urban Child Institute. 2014. "Self-Confidence Starts Early." Urban Child Institute. http://www.urbanchildinstitute.org/articles/features/self-confidence-starts-early

U. S. Department of Education. 1999. "Start Early, Finish Strong: How to Help Every Child Become a Reader." America Reads Challenge, U. S. Department of Education. https://www2.ed.gov/pubs/startearly/index.html

Wallace, Meri. 2012. "Simple Ways to Build Your Baby's Self-Esteem." *Psychology Today.* https://www.psychologytoday.com/blog/how-raise-happy-cooperative-child/201205/simple-ways-build-your-babys-self-esteem

Walton, Patrick. 2014. "Using Singing and Movement to Teach Pre-Reading Skills and Word Reading to Kindergarten Children: An Exploratory Study." *Language and Literacy* 16: 54–77.

Warnick, Melody. 2017. "Baby Speech Developmental Milestones." Parenting. http://www.parenting.com/article/baby-speech-milestones

Way, Jenni. 2005. "Number Sense Series: Developing Early Number Sense." NRICH Project. https://nrich.maths.org/2477

Weichman, Lauren. 2012. "Dressing Skills: Developmental Steps for Kids." North Shore Pediatric Therapy. http://nspt4kids.com/therapy/dressing-skills-developmental-steps-for-kids/

Weisleder, Adriana, and Anne Fernald. 2013. "Talking to Children Matters: Early Language Experience Strengthens Processing and Builds Vocabulary." *Psychological Science* 24(11): 2143–2152.

Welch, Graham. 2012. "The Benefits of Singing for Children." Researchgate.com. https://www.researchgate.net/profile/Graham_Welch/publication/273428150_The_Benefits_of_Singing_for_Children/links/550061710cf2d61f820d6e83/The-Benefits-of-Singing-for-Children.pdf

What to Expect. 2017. "Best Toys for Toddlers." What to Expect. https://www.whattoexpect.com/toddler/photo-gallery/best-toys-for-toddlers.aspx#01

What to Expect. 2017. "Why Push Toys Pay Off." What to Expect. https://www.whattoexpect.com/playroom/playtime-tips/push-toys.aspx

White, Burton. 1995. *The New First Three Years of Life*. New York: Fireside.

Wolfgang, Charles, Laura Stannard, and Ithel Jones. 2009. "Block Play Performance Among Preschoolers As a Predictor of Later School Achievement in Mathematics." *Journal of Research in Childhood Education* 15(2): 173-180.

Wonder Baby. n.d. "'Just One!' "The Beginnings of One-to-One Correspondence." Wonder Baby. http://www.wonderbaby.org/articles/just-one

Zangl, Renate. 2014. *Raising a Talker*. Lewisville, NC: Gryphon House.

Zero to Three. 2016. "Birth to 3 Months: Your Baby's Development." Zero to Three. https://www.zerotothree.org/resources/80-birth-to-3-months-your-baby-s-development

Index